A SEASONAL GUIDE TO THE FLOWER GARDEN

Ann Bonar

Marshall Cavendish · London New York Sydney

Editor: David Joyce
Designer: Elizabeth Rose
Illustrator: Barbara Howes

Published by Marshall Cavendish Books Limited
58 Old Compton Street
LONDON W1V 5PA

©Marshall Cavendish Limited 1980
First printing 1980
Printed in Great Britain by Ambassador College Press
ISBN 0 85685 803 X (hard-back)
        0 85685 807 2 (soft-back)

Contents

Introduction

The flower garden, large or small, can do more to enhance the exterior beauty of a home than any other feature. Carefully planned, it will provide year-round colour and greenery, at the same time as supplying the flower arranger with a constant source of material for indoor decoration. In this sense the flower garden covers not just annuals, perennials and bulbs, but lawns and the special features, such as rock gardens and ponds, which can give a garden its own particular character.

The one golden rule for success with the flower garden, as with all other aspects of gardening, is to work with the seasons. Following a rigid monthly schedule will not achieve this, for climate and weather do not perform according to such neat divisions, and it is they which effectively signal the change of the seasons and which, more particularly, govern the growth and development of plants.

Weather and climate are, of course, not the only factors. Good soil structure is vital. Almost certainly you will not have the ideal soil, a humus-rich loam containing a well-balanced mixture of plant foods. Even though you do not start with the ideal you can work towards it by adding compost and fertilizers. A regular supply of water is also a fundamental requirement for all plants. Going short of water means going short of food, too, so putting on all the fertilizers and manures will not help growth if there is not enough moisture.

Choosing the right position for the plants you want to grow is also an important key to success. Planting according to particular requirements for sun and shade and degree of shelter will give plants the chance they need to show their best. You should, of course, make sure you start with strong and healthy plants for these are much less likely to be seriously damaged by pests and disease. Remember, too, that general garden hygiene, such as tidying up garden rubbish, will reduce the chance of pests and diseases getting a hold.

A Seasonal Guide to the Flower Garden is not about the mysteries of gardening. Its theme is that the gardener's best wisdom is common sense and an appreciation of the role of the weather. Each season begins with a summary of things to do which is then followed by more detailed instructions on how to grow flowers and look after lawns and special features. In addition, there are useful charts and a section on Controls and Treatments.

THE FLOWER GARDEN
Early Spring

In early spring, there is a good deal that you can begin to do in the flower garden, unlike the kitchen garden, where the real work does not start until mid-spring. This season is one of the best for planting and transplanting herbaceous perennials and you can also deal with some bulbs, rock plants and plants grown from seed sown last year.

Although early spring can be treacherous in its weather, blowing hot and cold alternately, you can take advantage of a few mild days which help to dry the soil, and put in plants which, being hardy, will not be harmed if the weather then turns cold. The state of the soil is more important than the temperature; those with sandy soils can move plants more or less at will, but those who have to deal with sticky clays will do better to pick their time for planting, so that plant roots do not have to contend with rather too generous quantities of water. If you are doubtful about moving plants, remember that those with thick fleshy roots are the ones least likely to establish in wet soils.

Another of your main jobs will be getting the lawn into good condition after the winter rains and cold; the grass will start to grow again during the next few weeks and as soon as it does, you should begin the reviving treatment for both turf and soil.

Seed sowing outdoors can begin and the soil will need preparing for this; hardy annuals will be the main type of plant sown, though herbaceous perennials can also be grown from seed. Though they may take longer to become flowering plants than those perennials bought from garden centres and nurseries, they are considerably cheaper and you will be certain that they are strong and free of pests and diseases.

Half-hardy annuals and bedding-plant seeds can be sown in the greenhouse: in frames you can sow dahlias and sweetpeas in containers. Cuttings of various kinds can also be taken in the greenhouse.

At~a~glance diary

Prepare the soil for: sowing and planting outdoors

Sow seeds outdoors of: hardy annuals (see Table of Hardy Annuals in Early Summer)

Sow seeds under glass of: dahlia, herbaceous perennials, rock plants

Sow seeds under glass (in heat) of: half-hardy annuals and bedding plants (see Table in Mid-Winter)

Plant: biennials, herbaceous perennials, gladioli, montbretia, autumn-sown sweetpea

Divide: herbaceous perennials, snowdrop clumps

Lawn care: rake, brush, top, spike; treat moss with lawn and/or a proprietary moss-killer

Put to sprout: achimenes, large-flowered begonia, dahlia, gloxinia (sinningia)

Prick out: half-hardy annuals, begonia (fibrous-rooted and large-flowered), dahlia, gloxinia (sinningia), streptocarpus

Pot, topdress: greenhouse plants (foliage and summer-flowering kinds): e.g., asparagus, cacti, chlorophytum, ferns, fuchsia, hippeastrum, hoya, Italian bellflower jasmine, passion flower, pelargonium, succulents tradescantia, zebrina

Stop: late-flowering chrysanthemums

Increase: chrysanthemum, dahlia, fuchsia, pelargonium by cuttings

Greenhouse: ventilate; space out and protect young plants from sun

Weed and clear: over-wintering weeds, weed seedlings from amongst annual seedlings, beds, borders, rock gardens

Compost heap: use as mulch; start new heap

Jobs to do

Preparing the soil for outdoor sowing

The soil in beds and borders should be prepared for sowing seed as soon as it becomes workable. Drying winds and sun will hasten this condition and, when you find that it no longer sticks to your shoes, you can begin to fork the top few centimetres (inches) and break up the lumps. The initial deep digging should already have been done in autumn or early winter.

Remove stones and weeds as you fork and dust a dressing of superphosphate onto the soil surface as you work, making sure that it covers the area evenly. An average application rate is 45g per sq m ($1\frac{1}{2}$oz per sq yd).

Do this seed-bed preparation about ten days before you intend to sow, and then, on the actual day if possible, use a rake to level the surface and reduce the lumps of soil to an even smaller size, like crumbs. If done the day before, cover with plastic sheet overnight to protect from heavy rain.

Preparing the soil for outdoor planting

There is little work to be done here, as the bulk of it should have been done a few months ago and it is merely a case of forking the surface, removing weeds and other debris, and mixing in a general fertilizer dressing, preferably a slow-acting mixture, such as hoof and horn and bonemeal, or a 'straight' (e.g. dried blood), each at about 60g per sq m (2oz per sq yd). This is done about a week in advance of planting, to give the soil time to absorb the nutrients and so that plant roots do not come into direct contact with the fertilizer particles.

Sowing seed outdoors

Seeds to sow outdoors towards the end of early spring will be hardy annuals (see Early Winter for list). Since these are all hardy, there should be no difficulty in growing them, but of course the same rules for successful germination apply to these seeds as to any other – they must have moisture, a fine soil surface and, even if they are hardy, a temperature above freezing. So it will pay you to cover the soil in some way for a few days before sowing, with cloches, plastic sheet or tunnels to warm it up a little.

Scatter your seed evenly and thinly on soil which has been watered with a rosed watering can if the surface is dry and rake or sprinkle a very light covering of soil over the seed, so that it is covered to about twice its own depth. Protect from birds (see sowing grass seed, Mid-Spring).

A carefully planted rock garden in its full spring glory: iris, grape hyacinths, the Pasque flower, forget-me-nots and honesty combine beautifully.

Nothing is more evocative of spring-time than the primrose, whose pale yellow flowers bloom in both sun and shade.

You can also sow sweetpeas outdoors this month, in the place in which they are to flower. The trenches for them having been prepared in early winter, the seed should be sown 10cm (4in) apart and 5cm (2in) deep; you can sow a double, staggered row, with 25cm (10in) between the rows. However, sweetpea sowing at this time is somewhat of a last resort; results will not be as good as from autumn sowings and flowering will be much later, in mid-summer. For method of support, see staking, Mid-Spring.

Sowing seed under glass

If you have frames, or can acquire one or two and put them in a sunny sheltered place, you can sow dahlia seed in them, in boxes or pans. They will all be collections of mixed colours, not named cultivars, but they can be bedding dahlias or the normal larger, decorative kind. They need a temperature of about 13-16°C (55-60°F) to germinate, so you should wait until late in early spring before sowing in a frame; alternatively you can sow them in the greenhouse (without heat) or in a gently warmed propagator in the greenhouse.

Other seeds to sow in warmth will be half-hardy annuals and bedding plants. The earlier in the month you sow these seeds, the earlier they will flower, but whenever you sow them, the resultant plants should not be put outdoors until thoroughly accustomed to lower temperatures, and preferably after any likelihood of night frosts. If they have grown very large and have to be put outdoors before the weather is right, cloche protection will help to prevent actual damage, though they are likely to stop growing temporarily.

If you want to try your hand at growing herbaceous perennials and rock plants from seed, early spring is the best time to sow it, if you have glass protection. Artificial heat is not essential, though a little will hasten germination, but they are hardy plants – don't forget that most rock plants come from mountain sites where there can be snow into mid-spring, or even later.

Planting and dividing

The main plantings will be of herbaceous perennials, either of new plants, or of plants you already have, which need digging up, dividing and then replanting. This kind of plant grows well for three or four years, but then becomes straggly and does not produce as many or as good flowers. The centre of the crown becomes bare and the new growth appears round the edges, so that gaps start to appear, especially with such plants as golden rod (solidago), Michaelmas daisies and rudbeckias.

When you dig up the plants, lift them with as much of the root intact and unbroken as possible, then pull the crown apart into several good sections, each with buds and/or new shoots on it. You will find that the parts with most life in them will tend to detach from the more or less dead central part. If the crown is very tough and thick, with a mass of tangled roots, you can lever it into sections or use a really sharp knife to cut through the crown, but not the roots – disentangle these by hand.

You can take the opportunity to clear the crowns of any weeds that may be infesting the roots, and to clear out debris such as old stalks, leaves, stones, and slugs and snails, which all provide shelter for disease and other pests.

Make the planting holes large enough to take the roots of the plants spread out, without cramping and doubling up; roots put in bent back on themselves suffer a kind of strangulation and although the plant may not actually die at once, it grows slowly and is permanently weakened so that it dies prematurely. Put the plants in to the same depth as they were, filling the hole with crumbled soil, firm it in with the heel, rake the surface and water in if there is unlikely to be rain within the next few hours.

The double-flowered Asiatic ranunculus, planted in spring, are in vivid bloom in early summer.

You can also dig up and divide snowdrops in early spring, as soon as they have finished flowering; they re-establish very quickly and suffer no harm from lifting while the leaves are still green. In fact, if left until autumn and then dug up and divided, they take much longer to recover, and may not flower in the winter following.

Sweetpeas which were sown in autumn can be planted in their permanent flowering positions, and staked at the same time (see staking, Mid-Spring). If you were unable to get biennials into their flowering beds last autumn, they should be moved as soon as possible this season.

Montbretias and gladioli are summer-flowering bulbs (technically corms) planted in early spring, preferably towards the end of it. Montbretias will do best if started into growth before planting, as begonias are, by putting them into damp peat in trays in a frame. As soon as they start to produce green tips and the beginnings of roots, plant them with 5cm (2in) of soil above them and about 10cm (4in) apart. They are very undemanding plants and although it is generally advised to divide them every three years, they will flower for at least twenty years without this. Well-drained soil, slightly starved growing conditions and a sunny place will give the best flowering.

Modern gladioli are varied as well as extremely pretty. There are three main groups of hybrids: the large-flowered, which are the best-known sort; the miniatures, or *primulinus* kind, which includes the Butterfly type; and the early-flowering *colvillei* hybrids; the last named are slightly tender and are therefore usually grown in pots, being planted in autumn and kept in a cool greenhouse for flowering in early to mid-spring. They can be planted outdoors, but only in really warm, sheltered places, and will then flower in early summer.

Gladioli are sun-lovers and lovers of dryish, or free-draining soil or compost; plant them 10cm (4in) deep and 15cm (6in) apart. You will get a succession of flowers if you plant them in batches, once every ten to fourteen days until the end of mid-spring. The large-flowered kinds should be planted in rows 30cm (12in) apart, the miniatures about 20cm (8in) apart.

Lawn treatment

The lawn at this time of the year always looks rather sorry for itself, thin, limp and messy with leaves and twigs. As the temperature rises and the grass starts to grow, you can help to revive it more quickly and strongly by raking, brushing, topping and spiking, in that order. This work results in aerating the soil and the turf and removing possible pests.

Use a springbok rake, rake first in one direction and then at right angles across this; next brush, using a stiff brush to bring the grass upright and then cut the grass. Set the mower blades high, so that the grass is left about 2.5cm (1in) long; a harder cut can be given at the next mowing. After cutting, with the collecting box on, spike the lawn – you can use an ordinary garden fork for this. To do any real good, the tines should penetrate 10cm (4in) deep, but 7.5cm (3in) is better than nothing. Do this all over the lawn, about 12 or 15cm (5 or 6in) apart.

Rolling a lawn, to keep it level, used to be considered essential but nowadays it is thought to do more harm than good, by compacting the soil, especially since modern mowers have a roller fitted automatically. If there is moss on the lawn, raking should not be done until the moss has been treated, since raking only serves to spread it.

Treating moss on lawns

Moss thrives in damp conditions; it will spread rapidly in wet weather, but it will also appear where the soil is extremely acid, where it is compacted and lacking in air and where it is lacking plant food. In all these conditions, the lawn grasses become weak and cannot compete with invaders. Moss can be burnt out with lawnsand bought ready-mixed, or made up at home of 3 parts sulphate of ammonia, 1 part calcined (burnt) ferrous sulphate and 20

Bergenia, or 'elephant's ears', a neglected plant, flowers from mid-winter into early spring and even later. The glossy evergreen leaves are decorative in themselves.

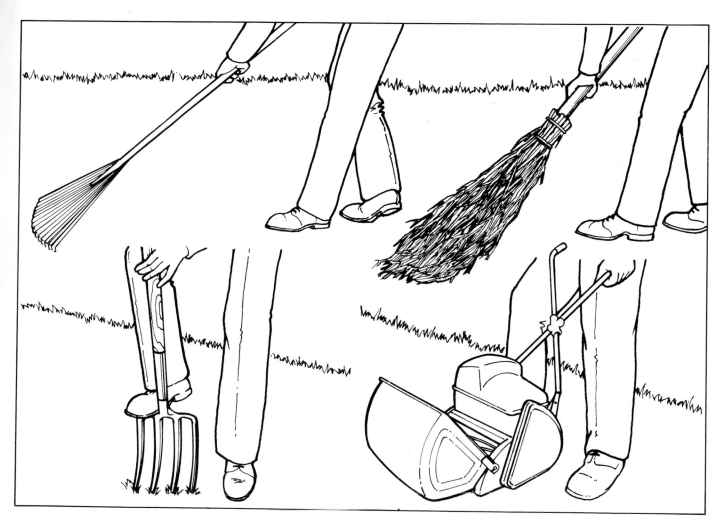

Rejuvenating the lawn after winter: rake with a springbok rake, brush thoroughly, 'top' the grass and aerate with a garden fork afterwards to a depth of about 10cm (4in). If the lawn has moss on it, do not rake until the moss has been treated: raking will spread it.

parts sand. This mixture is applied dry at 120g per sq m (4oz per sq yd); it must be put on evenly, otherwise the grass may be permanently damaged, and watered in if there is no rain after 48 hours. The grass is likely to be discoloured, brown or blackish, but this is temporary. When the moss is black and dead, then it can be raked away.

Proprietary moss killers containing mercury can also be used and there are one or two mercurized lawnsands available; the mercury will kill the moss spores as well as the vegetative growth.

However, for the permanent eradication of the moss, conditions for the growth of the grass must be put right and this means that you must ensure good soil aeration, an adequate food supply, frequent cutting to avoid the shock given by occasional very hard cutting, and a sufficient water supply in hot and/or dry weather. It is mostly summer droughts and watering long after it was first necessary that result in the invasion of the turf by coarse and weed grasses, weeds, moss and disease.

Sprouting

You can put achimenes, large-flowered begonias and gloxinias (sinningias) to sprout in moist peat if this was not done last month, but not in the propagator; the greenhouse will be sufficiently warm, if you are maintaining the minimum temperature. It is quite likely that some of them have already started to produce new shoots. Dahlias can be started as well, to provide shoots for cuttings. Take off any rotting tubers and put the healthy crowns in 15cm (6in) deep boxes, covering the tubers with moist peat or soil.

Pricking out

By now, the seeds sown last month in the propagator will be seedlings that need pricking out; they will include half-hardy annuals, and such slightly tender bedding and greenhouse plants as begonias (fibrous-rooted and large-flowered), dahlia, gloxinia (sinningia) and streptocarpus. In general, seedlings should be moved when they have two seed leaves and the first true leaf just appearing, in other words when they are large enough to handle. Lever them out, breaking the roots as little as possible, and drop each seedling into a hole in the compost which is large enough to prevent the roots being cramped, and deep enough to ensure that most of the stem is buried; the leaves should be just above the compost surface. Space them 5cm (2in) apart each way.

Quite often each seedling has a long main root or tap root; if you look closely at the tip of this, you will see that it finishes in a kind of rounded point, and it is there that the seedling takes in most of the food it needs. If that gets broken off, it will have to rely on the much less strong side roots to absorb food and may even have to grow a new root. While this is happening, it cannot absorb sufficient water, and this is why so many pricked out seedlings wilt as soon as they are moved. Clumsy lifting can damage a seedling so that the mature plant is never strong. Another important point in pricking out is to do it as soon as the seedling can be handled. The shock of moving is much greater when they are larger and there will be much more root to handle (and to damage); they may even have run short of food.

Snow-in-summer, Cerastium tomentosum, *flowers for several weeks and is good ground-cover but needs restricting.*

Once firmed into the compost, the seedlings should be gently watered with a rosed watering can and put in a shady place; a polythene tent over them will keep the atmosphere moist and help to stop any tendency to flag.

Potting and topdressing

Plants which are grown permanently in the greenhouse will need new compost every one or two years; if they are not particularly strong or fast growers, they can simply be topdressed, instead of completely repotted. Cuttings which were put to root last month may need potting into individual pots by now.

Plants to repot could include all foliage plants, such as tradescantia, zebrina, chlorophytum, asparagus and ferns, summer-flowering plants such as pelargoniums (geraniums), the Italian bellflower (*Campanula isophylla*), jasmine, fuchsia, hoya, cacti and other succulents, cobaea (cup-and-saucer plant) and passion flower (*Passiflora caerulea*).

In general, use a pot one size larger than the one the plant is in, and do not disturb the root-ball unless the roots have become very long, when they can be cut back to the root-ball, and the ball loosened a little. If the maximum size of the plant has been reached, use a pot the same size, but remove all the compost carefully from the roots, put a little new compost in the pot, and centre the plant on this, so that compost can be crumbled in evenly all round the roots.

When you repot, have the new compost ready in the greenhouse so that it is at the same temperature as that in which the plants are growing and use completely clean pots, plastic or clay. If new, clay pots should be put to soak in water for about twenty-four hours, otherwise they will absorb all the water you give to the compost which is intended for the plant and you will constantly be watering but getting poor plant growth. Put drainage material, such as pieces of broken clay pot, in the base of the clay pots, and then repot the plant.

Cacti can be difficult to handle because of their prickles; gloves will help and tongs are even better, the kind that form two halves of a ring, as they do least damage to the spines.

Pelargoniums which have been overwintered in the greenhouse can now be transferred to individual pots about 15 or 17.5cm (6 or 7in) in diameter, whatever size will take the roots without cramping them too much. Use the J.I. potting compost No. 2 with one part extra of coarse sand added, as pelargoniums like well-drained soils.

Topdressing consists simply of removing the top 2.5cm (1in) or so of compost and replacing it with fresh. Plants treated like this will need to have liquid feeding started much earlier than repotted plants. Hippeastrums can be started now if this has not already been done (see Late Winter).

Cuttings, such as early- and late-flowering chrysanthemums, which rooted last month, may also need potting now into their own pots. Pelargonium cuttings which were rooted last autumn can now also be transferred to larger pots.

Stopping

At some time during early spring, if not before, late-flowering chrysanthemums will have grown to about 15cm (6in) in height and should be stopped, to induce them to produce sideshoots and more flowers in due course. Stopping is a way of halting the upward growth of the main stem completely, and diverting the plant's energy into the production of side growths from the axil of the leaves. Most chrysanthemum cultivars tend to produce these growths in embryo, but they do not develop, unless the plant is stopped. To stop the plant, the growing tip and first pair of leaves are pinched off between finger and thumb.

Potting a rooted chrysanthemum cutting: use a 9cm (3½in) diameter pot, and put small pieces of crock, curve side upward, over the drainage hole. Fill in some of the potting compost, centre the roots on this and fill in compost round them, firming it at the sides with the fingers.

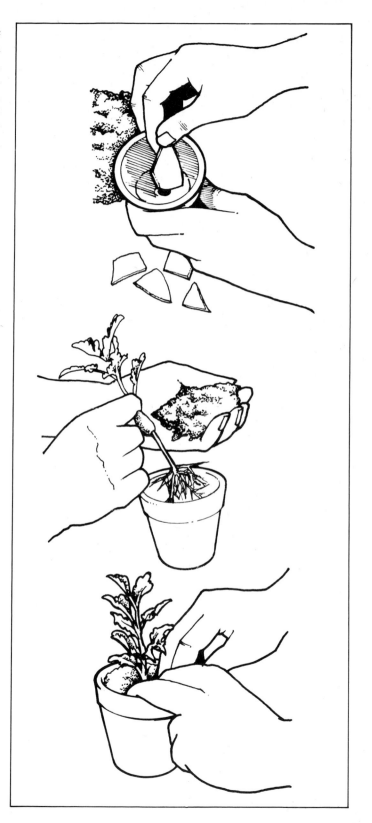

Increasing from cuttings

Cuttings to take and root in warmth in early spring include the early-flowering and the last of the late-flowering chrysanthemums (see Early Winter for method). Others include dahlias and fuchsias if new growth has started and pelargoniums – if these were not cut back last autumn – for flowering next winter in the greenhouse (see Early Autumn for method).

As with all 'soft-tip' cuttings, the ends of the new shoots should be used, while they are still green and soft and have not become hard and/or brown. Cut off a length of shoot about 7.5cm (3in) long, cutting just below a leaf or pair of leaves. Cut off the lowest leaves and put the cutting in the compost, so that half its length is buried. Make a sufficiently deep hole first with a dibber or pencil, against the side of the pot, and make sure the base of the cutting is resting on the compost at the bottom of the hole. Rooting occurs more quickly with cuttings placed at the side of the pot. Then fill in firmly with compost so that the cutting cannot be shifted with a gentle tug on a leaf. Water in, cover with a blown-up polythene bag and put in a warm shady place until the stem begins to lengthen, when rooting will have occurred. You can then take off the polythene bag.

Three or four cuttings can be put in a 9cm (3½in) diameter pot; hormone rooting powder can be used as an insurance. This method can be used for all soft-tip cuttings, no matter what the plant. Never use a shoot which has a flower or flower-bud on it, as it will not root.

Greenhouse management

Since the outside temperature is rising and plants are beginning to grow, you can dispense with artificial heat on sunny days, though it will still be necessary at night. Ventilation can be increased during the day and condensation should cease to be a problem. Pricked-out seedlings and potted cuttings will need spacing out as they grow, to avoid their becoming drawn; the need for water will steadily increase and germinating seeds must have an eye kept on them constantly, to avoid sunburn, drought and overcrowding because the pricking out has not been done quickly enough.

Weeding and tidying

In early spring, most weeding will be a matter of clearing off any weeds that have managed to survive the winter after a late germination last autumn; however, lawn weeds are best left until late in mid-spring. Where seeds are sown outdoors, weed seedlings should be dealt with as soon as they become obvious.

Beds and borders will need tidying to remove leaves, twigs and other debris. Rock gardens especially can be very messy after the winter: some plants need cutting back to remove dead growth, the soil needs forking lightly with a hand fork, and grit or gravel replaced where rain has washed it away. If conditions are dry enough, you can burn off the dead leaves and stems of pampas grass, otherwise cut them off and rake out debris from round the plants.

Compost heap

Last year's compost heap can be used as a mulch for permanent plantings, if a mulch was not given in the autumn, otherwise it can be kept for later use. A new heap can be started with this year's weeds and grass cuttings (see Mid-Spring for method of making).

Plants in flower

Anemone, Bergenia, Crocus, Chionodoxa, Doronicum, Eranthis (Winter aconite), Hyacinth, Iris unguicularis (syn. I. stylosa) Kingcup (caltha), Lenten rose (Helleborus orientalis), Polyanthus, Primrose, Primula (in variety), Pulmonaria (lungwort), Saxifraga (in variety), Scilla, Tulip (species)

Greenhouse

Cineraria, Freesia, Lachenalia, Primula (from early summer sowing), Schizanthus, Hyacinth (gently forced), Narcissi (gently forced), Tulip (gently forced)

Mid~Spring

This season can be one in which plants really start to grow, so that you can be very busy, both outdoors and in the greenhouse. Sometimes, on the other hand, new growth is slower to appear and extend, because the weather is dry and cold with east winds, although sunny. Flowers appearing at this time will last longer, but growing plants from seed outdoors can be more difficult than in early spring. Although half-hardy annuals can be sown outside towards the end of mid-spring, it is often better not to be in too much of a hurry with them and to wait until late spring.

Planting is safer, but even so, herbaceous perennials may need aftercare in the form of watering, though summer droughts are a long way off. Rock garden plants will not mind chilly conditions if these occur, but their more fragile roots will affect their ability to absorb water, so they will also need watching.

Another major job in mid-spring is making a lawn from seed; this is one of the best times to sow grass seed, especially for colder regions where autumn-sown grass seed is less likely to produce a good lawn. Here again, germination can be dodgy, as it is quite possible to sow grass seed and then not have it germinate for three weeks, because of lack of rain.

You will find that conditions in the greenhouse are getting rather crowded, if you have let your enthusiasm run away with you. Seeds will be germinating, seedlings will need pricking out, pricked-out plants will need potting, so will rooted cuttings, new growth will be providing cutting material, and plants put to sprout will need potting. Provided the temperature is rising outdoors, some of these can go into frames, but if it remains cold, you will have to do some expert juggling and fitting in.

Insect pests of all kinds will be hatching or emerging from winter dormancy and a few diseases will begin to appear, quickly or slowly, depending on the temperature. Be ready to deal with these, if they look like getting out of hand.

At-a-glance diary

Prepare the soil for: sowing seed and planting outdoors

Prepare compost for: sowing seed and potting under glass

Sow seeds outdoors of: hardy annuals (see Table of Hardy Annuals in Early Summer); also some of the half-hardy and bedding plants: dahlia,

Sow seeds under glass of: nasturtium, salpiglossis, ursinia, xeranthemum (everlasting) and zinnia; lawn grasses half-hardy annuals and bedding plants (see Table in Mid-Winter)

Plant outdoors: allium, crinum, gladioli, herbaceous perennials, montbretia, rock garden plants, autumn-sown sweetpea if not done in early spring

Thin: seedlings from seed sown outdoors in early spring

Lawn care: mow new lawns grown from seed; mow and feed established lawns

Stake, train and tie in: sweetpea

Compost heap: continue to make

Weed: annual flower and lawn grass seedlings, herbaceous beds and borders, paths

Prick out: half-hardy annuals and bedding plants sown in early spring, seedlings in frames

Pot: achimenes, begonia, chrysanthemum, gloxinia pelargonium, pricked out seedlings, streptocarpus, plants permanently in pots and not repotted in early spring

Stop: early-flowering chrysanthemum

Increase: chrysanthemum, dahlia, delphinium, fuchsia from cuttings

Greenhouse: water and ventilate

Jobs to do

Preparing the soil for sowing seed outdoors
One of the bigger jobs to do in the spring is producing a lawn from seed. The soil should have been thoroughly dug in autumn or early winter and most of the weeds removed. Now it needs a final cleaning up, about a week before you intend to sow, by forking the top few centimetres (inches) to remove weeds and rubbish, and to break up large lumps of soil. Add a compound fertilizer dressing with an analysis of about 7:7:7 (see Mid-Winter) when you do the forking. A week later, on the day you sow, you can rake to make the soil surface really fine and to do some rough levelling, and then make a finished level, using a line, pegs, boards and a spirit level. Once you are sure there are no bumps and hollows, tread the seed-bed to consolidate it lightly, and give a final raking, standing on boards, to produce the right tilth.

Seed-beds for flowering plants can also be prepared now, as in early spring.

Preparing compost for sowing seed under glass
If you did not have time to make up compost in late winter or early spring, it should be mixed as soon as possible so that it has a little time, at any rate, to blend together.

Preparing the soil for planting outdoors
Much of the planting in mid-spring is the same as in early spring, with some additions, so you can follow the instructions given in that season, and make sure that any fertilizer added goes on a few days in advance of planting.

Preparing compost for potting under glass
As with the seed composts, so potting composts need to be made early in mid-spring and left in the greenhouse to warm up to the same temperature as the one in which the plants are growing.

Sowing seed outdoors
Grass seed should be sown fairly early in mid-spring; it takes about seven to ten days to germinate and perhaps

There are water-lilies in many colours besides the usual white, and types to suit all pools, whether shallow or deep.

another ten to fourteen before the first cut can be made. A windless day is best; marking out the area in square metres (yards) with lines will help you to make sowing more even.

Average rate for sowing seed is about 45-60g per sq m (1½-2oz per sq yd), using the higher rate if birds are likely to be a nuisance or germination conditions a bit problematical. Another way of ensuring evenness of sowing,

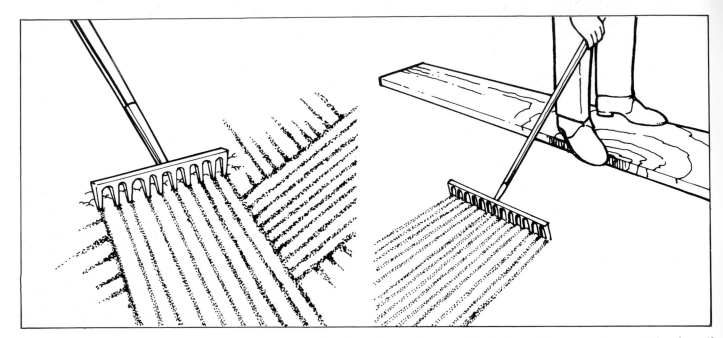

when doing it by hand, is to sow half the seed in one direction and the remainder at right angles to it. This evenness of sowing is important, otherwise you will start with a patchy lawn, and subsequently you will never be able to produce an evenly thick sward. Large areas can be sown with a fertilizer distributor, to which a metering roller for sowing seeds is attached. Again, two half sowings are advisable.

After sowing, a very light raking, then cross-raking, can be done to give the best results, though if time is short, this can be dispensed with. Finally, bird inhibitors can be put on or, on small areas, black cotton strung above the soil. Seed treated against birds can be bought, but loses its viability quickly, so should be used in the season for which it was intended and not kept for later use.

Hardy annuals can be sown this month with more chance of a good display later on; germination in early spring can be risky due to treacherous weather conditions. You can add to those suggested for early spring: aster, dahlia, layia (tidy tips), nasturtium, nicotiana, salpiglossis, sweet sultan, ursinia, xeranthemum (everlasting flowers) and zinnia. It is not quite too late for sweetpeas but those sown now will not flower until late summer.

If you have a nursery bed, which is really rather indispensable for flower as well as vegetable gardening, you can also sow seed now of bulbs such as crocus, lilies and snowdrops and of herbaceous perennials and rock plants, giving the seeds cloche protection if the temperature is down to freezing at night. Sow as thinly as possible, especially the bulbs.

Preparing a seed-bed for sowing a new lawn. Rake the soil surface to a fine crumb-like consistency, standing on a board, and then rake crosswise for final levelling and evenness.

Sowing seed under glass

In the greenhouse you can sow the same half-hardy annuals and bedding plants as last month but, unless the weather is very cold, you should be able to do without artificial heat during the day. You can also sow cobaea and ipomoea, and freesia for flowering during autumn and early winter. Cobaea and ipomoea have rather large seeds and grow quickly once they have germinated, so sowing them singly in 5cm (2in) pots, preferably peat pots, makes it easier to deal with their first potting.

Ipomoea in particular does not like its roots being disturbed; if they are, the first two or three true leaves tend to turn yellow and then white, the plant ceases to grow and eventually dies. This yellowing will also appear if the young plants are kept in bright sunlight or if the temperature drops below 16°C (60°F). They do need to be kept really quite warm, both in the compost and air temperature and if you can supply a temperature of nearer 21°C (70°F), so much the better.

Freesias can easily be grown from seed, and if it is sown now in a temperature of 16°C (60°F), the first flowers will start to appear in mid-autumn. They grow an unusually long taproot, so the deeper the container the better; the depth should be at least 17.5cm (7in). Use a compost containing soil, such as J.I. potting No. 3, and sow the seeds spaced 2.5cm (1in) apart and at the same depth. A 23cm (9in) pot will take about nine or ten seeds. The leaves and stems tend to be rather long and straggly, especially the stems, so 37.5cm (15in) long split canes with string threaded across them should be provided for support. Place them round the container edge and in the centre, so that the plants grow up through a supporting network. After germination, the temperature can be lowered a little.

Planting outdoors

As in early spring, you can plant or lift and divide herbaceous plants, but it is advisable to do this as early in the month as possible, as growth will really be getting under way.

This is the best time to plant rock garden plants as well, preferably when they have just finished flowering, though they can be moved or planted successfully while in flower. You must then do it quickly, with as little damage to the roots as possible, water them in and make quite sure they do not want for water while establishing. Cool, moist weather conditions are best.

Violets can be planted now, either bought plants, or crowns from your own plants. Crowns are pieces separated from a parent plant, each with plenty of roots. Violets thrive if planted where they are protected from summer sun at midday and given a moist, humus-rich soil. They must be watered in after planting, unless rain is imminent. If you see any signs of violet midge trouble, pick off the affected leaves (see Flower Garden Controls and Treatment section).

Gladioli can be planted during mid-spring, at intervals of a week or so to provide a succession of flowers; allium, crinum and montbretia can all be planted at the beginning of the season. Alliums tend to prefer a sunny place and gritty soil and, given these, some species will naturalize so well that they become a nuisance.

Crinum × powellii produces beautiful deep pink, lily-like flowers in late summer and autumn; its large bulbs should be planted 15cm (6in) deep and about 23cm (9in) apart. A well-drained soil, to which plenty of rotted organic matter was added in winter, is required, and a sunny place at the foot of a south or west-facing wall. Once planted, it can be left alone for many years, provided it is mulched each spring. Planted with agapanthus, the blue African lily which likes much the same conditions, the resulting combination of flower colour is very pretty.

In spite of its name, the Skunk Cabbage, Lysichitum americanum, *does not smell and is a handsome waterside plant.*

Thinning

The seeds sown outdoors in early spring will need thinning some time during the next few weeks. Thinning means removing some of the seedlings which have germinated, to allow the remainder enough space to grow and mature fully. It should be done when they are just large enough to handle, to leave roughly 5cm (2in) between each remaining seedling; thin a second time when they have produced five or six true leaves, so that there is about 10-20cm (4-8in) between the plants, depending on their final height.

The wild white daisy has been bred and selected so that strains of seed will now produce double rose-pink flowers.

Mowing

A new lawn which has been grown from seed may need its first cut by the end of mid-spring, if conditions for germination and growth have been good. The grass blades will then be about 5cm (2in) long. Before cutting, you can roll it once, with a light roller, to firm the roots of the young plants into the soil. Set the mower blades high, make sure they are razor sharp and then take only the top off the grass, about 1cm ($\frac{1}{2}$in).

Mowing of an established lawn can get into full swing, as the grass will be growing quickly, and you can reduce the height of cut to 0.5-1cm ($\frac{1}{4}$-$\frac{1}{2}$in) by the beginning of late spring. Mow the lawn with the collecting box attached, otherwise the clippings will choke the sward. Hot, dry weather is the only time the mowings can be left; they will then conserve moisture. If you have time, brushing with a stiff broom before you mow will maintain good aeration of the turf and prevent the build-up of a mat of vegetation on the soil surface.

Feeding

Established lawns can be fed, using a compound lawn fertilizer or, if you want quick but not long-lasting results, sulphate of ammonia, 15g ($\frac{1}{2}$oz) in 4.5L (1 gal) of water, put on with a spray or with a watering-can with a rose. Dry fertilizer must be put on evenly, at the rate recommended by the manufacturers, as a patchy application will only result in burning the grass and quite possibly killing it. Another requirement is moist soil, with the chance of rain within a few hours.

Staking, training and tying

Sweetpeas planted in early spring after being overwintered will begin to elongate rapidly and should be supplied with 2.5m (8ft) stakes, such as bamboo canes, one to each stem, to which they can be attached with sweetpea rings. Attach twine or wire to the tops of the canes along the row and support each end cane with a strong stake. Tendrils and side-shoots should be taken off as they appear. Tendrils take the place of a leaflet; side-shoots grow from the join between the main stem and a leaf stem. There is more about the training of sweetpeas in Early Summer.

Compost heap

The new one can be started in earnest, as weeds germinate along with your hardy annuals and new lawn. Give it a base of brushwood or bricks spaced well apart, so that air can get underneath, and surround it with a wooden framework, straw bales, rigid plastic, or black plastic sheet. Build it 120-150cm (48-60in) high, about the same width and any convenient length. Sticking a pole in the centre will ensure that there is a kind of chimney going through the heap, up which air can be drawn when you withdraw the pole at the finish of building.

Weeding

The main weed problem will be in the annual beds and patches and on the seed-bed provided for your new lawn. If both areas were not properly fallowed, there will be as many, if not more, weed seeds as cultivated seedlings, germinating merrily and growing faster. You can water on a solution of a new lawn weedkiller about a week after the grass germinates, otherwise you will have to remove the worst weeds by hand. However, with large areas this is impracticable, but usually as the grass grows and is cut, the weeds will be overcome, as these annual kinds cannot compete with the grass and withstand frequent cutting at the same time.

Amongst the annuals, handweeding will be necessary and with the smaller areas is quite practicable. Elsewhere in the garden, hoeing or handweeding will keep aliens at bay, if your perennials and groundcovers are not sufficiently closely planted to prevent their obtaining a toe-hold.

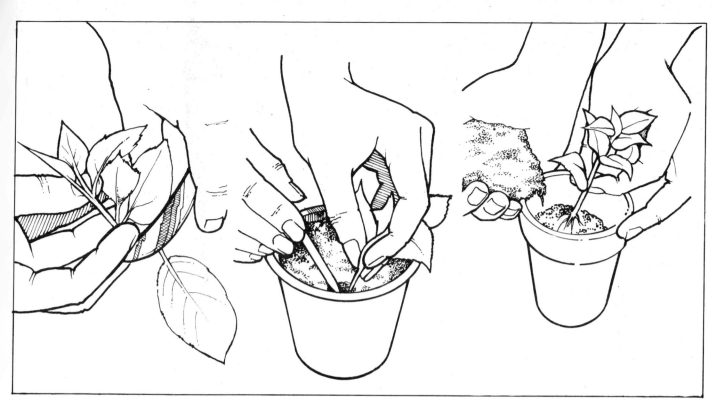

This is a good time of the year to eradicate weeds on paths; you can either water them with a weedkiller which lasts for six months, or you can remove them by hand and then apply one which lasts a year (see Flower Garden Treatments and Controls section).

Pricking out

The half-hardy annuals and bedding plants sown in artificial heat two or three weeks ago will need to be pricked out into boxes. Seeds sown in frames may have germinated sufficiently well for these seedlings also to need pricking out (see Early Spring for method).

Potting

The corms and tubers that you started in early spring in moist peat can be transferred to individual pots, 12.5-17.5cm (5-7in) in diameter for all but the achimenes. Do not completely bury the tuber or corm and use a rather peaty compost. Achimenes can be very slow to sprout but when the shoots are about 5cm (2in) tall, transfer the tubercles to 15 or 17.5cm (6 or 7in) pots and plant them about 7.5cm (3in) apart. At the same time, put in 15cm (12in) long split canes for the upright growing kinds.

Rooted cuttings such as those of early- and late-flowering chrysanthemums and pelargoniums can be potted

Making a soft tip cutting: The tip of a new young shoot is cut off cleanly below a leaf or pair of leaves so that it is about 7.5-10cm (3-4in) long. The lowest leaves are removed, the cutting half-buried in a hole in the compost at the side of the pot and firmed well in. When rooted, the cutting is grown on in its own pot in good potting compost.

or potted on. Be guided by the state of the roots; if they have filled the soil ball and are just spreading round the outside, the plants are ready for new pots, about 2.5-4cm (1-1½in) in diameter larger than the old ones. Roots coming through the drainage hole or wound round and round the base mean the plant is long overdue for a larger pot.

Late-flowering chrysanthemums, if the cuttings were taken in early or mid-winter, may be ready to go into their final pots, 23cm (9in) in diameter. Use J.I. potting compost No. 3. Such potting is likely to be necessary at the end of mid-spring (see Late Spring for method).

Pricked-out seedlings may also need to be moved into their first pots, using a size which the roots can fit into comfortably without being cramped. If they have one or two long roots, with plenty of shorter, finer ones, it does no harm to shorten the long ones to a convenient length.

Repot or topdress those plants permanently in containers which were not done in early spring.

Stopping

Early-flowering chrysanthemums can be stopped in the same way and for the same reasons as late-flowering kinds (see Early Spring).

Increasing

Dahlias, fuchsias and delphiniums can be propagated from cuttings. The dahlias put to sprout in early spring should have long enough shoots by now to provide cuttings; use those about 5-7.5cm (2-3in) long. If you cut them off to leave a stub, this will produce more shoots later on.

Fuchsia cuttings can be made in the same way from the newly produced shoots (see Early Spring for method). Outdoor delphiniums should also have sprouted by now and, if the slugs have left any, the same length cuttings can be made from the shoots and put in sandy compost in the frame. It may still be possible to take cuttings of early-flowering chrysanthemums.

Watering

Greenhouse plants will be needing more and more water; there are various ways of doing this according to the equipment and time you have available.

Ventilating

Continue to increase the ventilation in the greenhouse as the weather gets warmer. Turn the heat off when possible, but make sure the seedlings and rooted cuttings do not catch a chill. Frame lights can be raised during the day, or removed altogether in sunny weather.

Treating pests and diseases

Mid-spring sees the big hatch of insect pests, especially greenfly, the universal pest of plants. Other sucking insect pests such as leaf suckers and leaf-hoppers also appear from tiny overwintering eggs on weeds, bushes and trees, and caterpillars of all kinds will begin to eat leaves, as well as stems and, eventually, flowers. Leatherjackets may make a final onslaught on lawn grasses before they pupate – they account for pale brown patches of dead grass on many lawns in spring. Diseases will not be quite so troublesome for a while yet, apart from grey mould (*Botrytis cinerea*), but peonies will need watching for blight and bud disease at this time (see Flower Garden Controls and Treatment section).

Cosmos is a freely-flowering annual for sowing outdoors in spring to flower from mid-summer. It comes from Mexico and grows and flowers best in a sunny place and poor soil.

Plants in flower

Anemone, Arabis, Aubrieta, Bluebell, Chionodoxa, Crocus, Daffodil, Forget-me-not, Grape hyacinth, Hyacinth, Kingcup (caltha), Lamium maculatum, Lenten rose (Helleborus orientalis), Lithospermum, Narcissus, Polyanthus, Primrose, Primula, Scilla, Tulip, Violet

Greenhouse

Calceolaria, Hippeastrum, Lachenalia, Primula obconica, Schizanthus

Late Spring

The season of late spring is probably the busiest one of the year in the flower garden. It is an in-between time; the spring display is finishing and these plants need to be tidied up and allowed to rest. Those which are coming on to take their place will be growing fast and will need constant attention. You will also be able to start off some of next year's spring-flowering plants. The grass will be growing so rapidly that the lawn will need cutting every week.

In late spring there can be a slow but steady rise in temperature. By now, winter is definitely over, though there may be strong cold winds blowing through the whole period, but in sunny sheltered gardens some days can be really hot. The night temperature is the important one now and a constantly low one, even sometimes down to freezing, explains why some plants and seedlings are very slow to grow. This is where cloches and frames are so useful for protecting and bringing plants on so that they are ready for the hot weather.

There will be some soil preparation to do outdoors for sowing and planting; late spring is the best time to plant submerged water plants, including water lilies. The scene in the greenhouse can also be fairly active, with pricking out, sowing and potting all to be done, for summer displays of exotic plants and for flowering next winter and early spring. The greenhouse will need even more care with temperature control, and watering will be increasingly necessary.

Watchfulness will be the key word for pests and diseases. Greenfly and caterpillars will be the most annoying of these in general, though on certain plants there will be specific troubles through the season: capsid bugs on chrysanthemums, earwigs on dahlias, mildew on Michaelmas daisies or rust on antirrhinums. Birds are occasionally a nuisance, but not nearly to the same extent as they are on vegetables and fruit.

At~a~glance diary

Prepare the soil for: sowing seed and planting outdoors

Prepare compost for: sowing seed and potting under glass

Sow seeds outdoors of: hardy and half-hardy annuals (see Table in Early Summer and Mid-Winter): biennials, Canterbury bells, double daisies, foxglove, hollyhock

Sow seeds under glass of: cacti, cineraria, cobaea, ipomoea

Plant outdoors: allium; half-hardy annuals and bedding plants; crinum, dahlia, gladioli; herbaceous perennials; pansy, rock plants, water and waterside plants

Prick out: half-hardy annuals and bedding plants

Pot: chrysanthemum, dahlia, delphinium, fuchsia, pelargonium grown from cuttings; half-hardy annuals and bedding plants if getting large; greenhouse plants permanently in pots that are ready; cobaea, ipomoea

Thin: hardy annuals

Harden off: freesia, half-hardy annuals and bedding plants

Lift: spring-flowering bulbs if site is needed for summer bedding

Rest: freesia, lachenalia, any outdoor spring-flowering bulbs which have been brought on early in pots

Stake, train: delphinium, erigeron, euphorbia, lupin Michaelmas daisy, peony, poppy and pyrethrum outdoors; achimenes, begonia, freesia and climbing plants indoors

Jobs to do

Preparing the soil for sowing seed outdoors

You will need to fork and rake the soil into a good condition for sowing various seeds, mostly in beds and borders, and it should be much easier to do than it was earlier in the spring. A section of the nursery bed will need to be prepared for seeds as well. In all cases, do try to make sure the seed-bed is level and evenly firm, otherwise you will have patchy germination and weak plants. Hollows and bumps mean that seeds are washed by rain into clumps, and soil which has been firmed too thoroughly will be badly drained.

Preparing compost for sowing seed under glass

This in fact may have already been done, if you made up a good quantity in mid-spring. If you are short of time, you can use ready-made John Innes Seed Compost. If not, follow the details for seed-compost preparation given in Late Winter.

Preparing the soil for planting outdoors

As with early and mid-spring, soil preparation consists of forking and removal of weeds, stones and general rubbish. Also, it is a good idea to add compound fertilizer if you are going to grow chrysanthemums and dahlias or if your soil tends to be the quick-draining type. Plant foods are washed through the latter before the plant roots can absorb them.

Since water plants, water lilies in particular, usually are best planted in pools during late spring, the sites or baskets should be prepared now. You will get the best results if you can plant direct into the pool bottom, but this does mean emptying the pool completely. If you do this, spread a layer about 12.5 or 15cm (5 or 6in) deep of good loam all over the pool base and firm it down well.

Alternatively, you can plant the aquatics which grow under water and up through it in baskets, filling them with good loam put through a 1cm ($\frac{1}{2}$in) sieve. Bonemeal mixed with this at the rate of 60g (2oz) per container will supply long-lasting food. Prepare this mixture about a week before you intend to plant.

Preparing compost for potting under glass

Potting composts may again be necessary, depending on what you are growing; there are all sorts of plants which can go into their final containers in late spring and you may need a good deal (see Late Winter for recipes and quantities).

Sowing seed outdoors

Seeds to sow in the open are half-hardy annuals, annuals if you are behind (they should produce a display but late in the summer), and biennials for next spring, such as Canterbury bells, double daisies, foxglove, sweet william, *Verbascum bombyciferum* (mullein) and wallflower. Technically speaking, sweet williams are perennial, but are treated as biennials.

The half-hardy annuals will do best if you can put cloches over the seed-sowing site a few days in advance and then keep the cloches on at night until there is no longer any risk of frost.

If you can get the biennials sown now, they will be magnificent in spring next year as they will have had the longest possible growing season. Seed is sown in a seed-bed and the seedlings thinned and then transplanted to another part of the nursery bed to grow on through the summer until final planting in autumn.

This is the general method of cultivation but there are exceptions and, if you are short of time, it is possible to leave the young plants where they are, provided they have been well spaced out by thinning, until planting time in autumn. Verbascum is not transplanted at all, but planted direct from the seed-bed to its permanent position the spring after sowing. Hollyhocks, which are usually treated as biennials, can also be grown as perennials, though they tend to deteriorate rather rapidly.

Sowing seed under glass

In the greenhouse, seeds to sow now are some of those plants which flower in their pots next winter and spring, such as *Primula malacoides* and cineraria; cobaea and

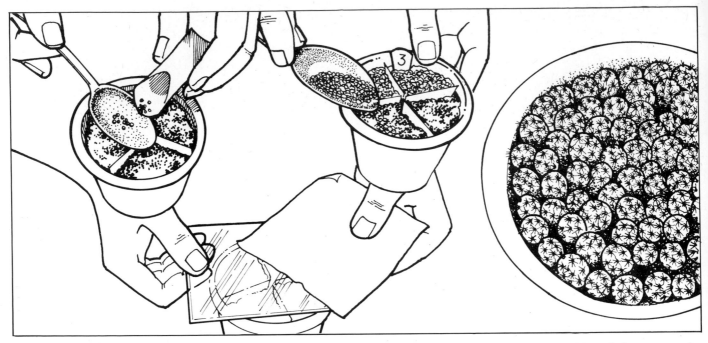

Sowing cactus seed: Use a pan with plenty of drainage material and very sandy compost; sow thinly and keep warm and covered until germinated. Prick out seedlings a year later.

ipomoea can also be sown for flowering later on this summer and in autumn, as can cactus seed, but the plants from these will not flower until next year at the earliest.

Cacti sown in late spring should germinate within about 7–14 days, but can be left in their seed containers until next spring as they are very slow to grow. Keep the seedlings in a little shade, otherwise the leaves discolour; when young, cacti do not like bright sunlight. Water occasionally but carefully.

Primula seed is very fine, difficult to sow and difficult to germinate. Mix it with sand for even sowing; use a sandy compost and a pan rather than a pot. Cover the seed with a light, fine covering of compost, then cover the pan with a piece of glass and put in a shaded place, making sure that the compost remains moist but not soggy. Temperature should be about 13-16°C (55-60°F). Germination may take several weeks and will be rather erratic when it does start.

Planting outdoors

Towards the end of late spring, you will be able to put out the bedding plants and half-hardy annuals, provided they have been well hardened-off in a frame. There is no point in planting earlier than this unless you have a sheltered garden; too often this kind of plant gets put out early in late

spring or even in mid-spring and, although it may not be killed as a result, it will be stunted and slow to grow so that no time is gained.

Choose a warm day, make sure the soil and the root ball are moist before planting and plant in the evening; warm them in lightly and cover with cloches if the temperature is below 10°C (50°F) at night. Spacing depends on the height and spread of the mature plant (see table, Mid-Winter) and can be between 10 and 45cm (4 and 18in).

Hardened-off rooted dahlia cuttings can similarly be planted in spring with cloche protection to start with, as dormant dahlia tubers which will be just starting to sprout. Spacing can be anything from 23-90cm (9-36in) apart, depending on whether the plants are bedding, the miniature pom-pom type or the giant-flowered decoratives. They will need good, large holes to take the roots or tubers comfortably, and stakes put in now will save a lot of worry later on. Dahlia top growth can be considerable and, although a single stout stake just behind the plant is sometimes sufficient, they often need several additional lighter ones on the outside, round which string can be tied. The stakes should be rammed firmly into the soil and need to extend at least 90cm (36in) above it for the taller varieties.

Submerged water plants – such as water lilies, pickerel and dwarf reedmace – can be planted now. You can also plant those that grow at the water's edge, or in mud or shallow water. The submerged aquatics can go into containers, with the crown just protruding above the compost surface. A layer of clean gravel or shingle on the surface will help to discourage fish from exploring the compost and keep the plant in position.

If you plant directly into loam, do it very firmly with the roots well spread out and anchor the crowns with a few stones as an extra insurance against floating. When you run the water in do so gradually, a few centimetres (inches) at a time, with about a week between additions, until the pool is full. Baskets can be lowered straight into their positions in the pool.

There is still time to plant allium and crinum (see planting, Mid-Spring), and the last of the gladioli (see planting, Early Spring). Pansies sown under glass in early spring will be ready for planting outdoors, after hardening off in a frame; they should begin to flower in late summer. The herbaceous perennials and rock plants grown from seed sown in early spring can also be planted where they are to grow, for flowering, in most cases, for the first time next summer.

Pricking out
By now, the half-hardy bedding plants and annuals sown in mid-spring will need transferring to trays of potting compost; a standard seed-tray will take about 25-30 seedlings.

Potting
The cuttings of dahlias and delphiniums may need one transitional potting before planting outdoors, into 7.5 or 10cm (3 or 4in) pots. Chrysanthemum, fuchsia and pelargonium cuttings can also be moved into pots. Fuchsias can go into a final pot size of at least 20cm (8in) diameter for flowering; pelargoniums will be satisfied with a 12.5-15cm (5-6in) diameter. Thereafter they will all remain in pots either in the greenhouse or outdoors in good summer weather.

The final potting for early and late-flowering chrysanthemums needs to be done with more care than usual, as the plants will be in their pots for anything from four to eight months and they will be growing vigorously and flowering profusely. They will need 23cm (9in) pots and J.I. potting compost No. 3; some gardeners make up a No. 4 mixture, for especially good blooms.

Pots, whether clay, plastic or whalehide, should be well crocked for best results and a little compost put on top **of** the crocks. The plants should be turned out of their present containers; if they are firmly entrenched a pointed stick pushed through the drainage hole should help to loosen them. Drainage material is removed from the base of the rootball and the plant set centrally in its new pot, so that the

One of the most handsome biennials, the foxglove is a lover of shade and moist soil, but it will grow in most sites.

surface of the rootball is 2.5-5cm (1-2in) below the pot rim. Compost is then poured in round it and rammed firmly down with a wooden rammer until the container is full. Firm, even potting is very important. Each plant should be given three bamboo canes, about 90-105cm (36-42in) long, spaced evenly round the edge of the pot. Finish by watering and standing the plants in a sheltered place free from the midday sun for a few days, after which they will take any amount of sun.

The half-hardy annuals and bedding plants sown in warmth in early spring and then pricked out may need small pots by now; they can be kept in these pots if the weather is cold and wet, but should be accustomed to lower temperatures ready for planting outdoors late in late spring or at the beginning of early summer.

Thinning
The hardy annuals sown outdoors last month are the group of plants that will need thinning now. It is important to do it while they are still tiny, otherwise they quickly become straggly, lie about on the soil and never grow into the stout plants that will provide the display expected of annuals.

Hardening off
As soon as freesia seedlings are showing about 1-2.5cm (½-1in) of leaf, they can be moved into a cold frame and hardened off for two weeks or so. Then stand them in the open, in a cool, lightly shaded place for the summer; too much warmth will delay flowering.

Half-hardy annuals and bedding plants, whether pricked out or potted, can be put in a frame also, to become gradually accustomed to lower temperatures. Increase ventilation until no protection is supplied, even at night, unless the temperature drops below 10°C (50°F).

Lifting bulbs
The spring-flowering bulbs such as daffodils, crocus, hyacinth and tulips will have finished flowering or be nearly finished and, if they are growing outdoors, can be treated in one of two ways.

If the ground in which they are growing is not wanted for summer plants, they can be left where they are and the leaves allowed to die naturally. The leaves will manufacture some of the food the bulb needs to develop its flower embryo for next spring. Daffodils have actually produced this embryo by the end of late spring and if the leaves are cut off to tidy up the bulbs or because they were growing in the lawn, flowering is unlikely. Such bulbs will often produce offsets instead.

If you have spring bulbs growing where you have planned a display of summer bedding, you can dig up the bulbs as soon as flowering is over and replant them at once in a spare, slightly shaded corner. The technique is to dig a shallow trench and lay the bulbs in at an angle, so the leaves are lying on the soil surface; fill in the trench with crumbled soil and then water if at all dry. This is known as 'heeling in'. Provided the roots have not been badly damaged in the process of digging up, the bulbs will suffer no harm and will continue to ripen. Once the leaves have withered completely, they can be dug up at any time and eventually replanted. Whatever you do, remove the flower heads when they have died, unless you want the seed.

Resting bulbs
Bulbs growing in the greenhouse which flowered through early and mid-spring will also be coming up to their resting and ripening time. These could include freesia, hyacinth, lachenalia, narcissi and tulip, in fact any of the outdoor spring bulbs which you may have brought on for early display.

Watering should continue while the leaves remain green but as soon as the tips begin to turn yellow, the quantity and frequency of watering should be gradually decreased. When the leaves have completely withered, no more watering should be done. It does no harm to liquid feed with a potash-high fertilizer during and after flowering, but this is not necessary once the plants start to die down. When growth has finished, the containers can be put under the greenhouse staging, laid on their sides for the summer.

Freesias are, however, an exception. These should be removed from the compost; you will find, when doing this, that the corms have buried themselves much deeper than the seed was originally sown. There will be one large and several smaller corms to each plant and, unless you want to go into the business of freesias as cut flowers, it is best to keep the largest corms only and do away with the remainder. You could grow them on, but it takes two to five years to produce flowering corms, depending on their size, and you will need a great deal of compost and space if you do decide to raise freesias in this way.

Clean the corms you are keeping of compost, roots and dead leaves, lay them in a single layer in a seed tray and store them in the dark, ideally in a temperature between 19 and 30°C (68 and 86°F). Too high a temperature or storage in sun results in 'petrified' corms; too low a temperature produces 'sleepers', which do not flower but which also do not die. They will grow normally if planted the following summer, having missed a year.

Staking/training

The herbaceous perennials will be growing fast and many of them will need supports. There are just as many that can be grown without staking (see tables, Early and Mid-Autumn), but the older, more popular perennials usually need some support. Amongst these latter are delphinium, erigeron, some euphorbias, lupin, peony, poppy, pyrethrum and Michaelmas daisies if growth is well enough advanced.

Bushy twigs like pea sticks, bamboo canes, stakes such as those which are used for dahlias and extending wire rings are some of the supports available, used in conjunction with fillis (soft string), plastic-covered wire, sweetpea rings or twist-ties. If put on when growth is about 30cm (12in) high and the stems attached so that the plants do not look bundled up and can grow naturally, the supports should be quickly masked by leaves.

Some of the lilies may also need staking; a single cane is sufficient for one plant. Chrysanthemums, dahlias and sweetpeas will already have been staked when planted or sown.

Indoor plants with growth which may be long enough to need support include achimenes, begonias, freesias from seed and climbers. The pendula begonias and some achimenes are natural trailers, very good for growing in hanging baskets. Most pot plants can be staked with split bamboo canes but there are special, extending, wire stakes for the double-flowered begonias; they finish in a kind of cup or half ring on which the flowers rest. Because their length can be manipulated, they can be used for a variety of begonias.

Sweetpeas will need frequent attention every three or four days, to remove tendrils, attach the stems to the supports and remove sideshoots. There is more detail – and a line illustration – covering this aspect of the care of sweetpeas in Early Summer, in Tying/Training.

Various methods of staking plants. Left: *This shows one of the best ways of staking dahlias, with a tripod of stout stakes on the outside of the plants.* Right: *Twiggy brushwood is suitable for many border perennials.*

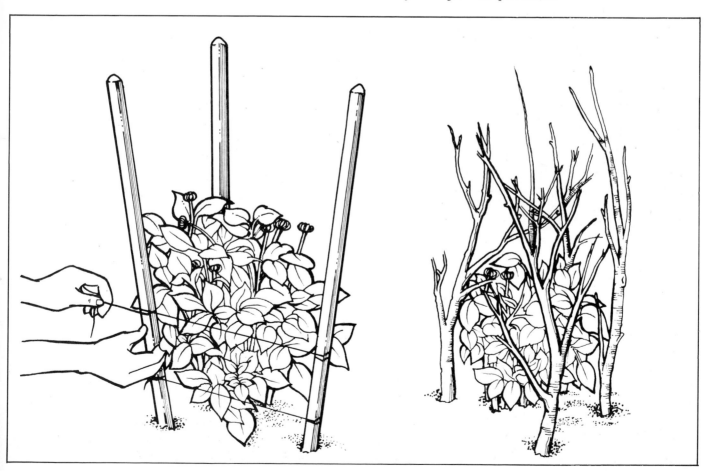

Cutting back/deadheading

The remains of flowers should be removed from spring-flowering bulbs and herbaceous perennials. Rock plants such as aubrieta can be trimmed with shears and this treatment, far from being brutal, in fact clears out 'dead wood' to such an extent that some flower a second time, especially if encouraged with a little feeding after cutting.

Feeding

Hippeastrums which have finished flowering and are now ripening their bulbs will be encouraged to flower next year if given a liquid fertilizer with a higher potassium content than nitrogen and phosphorus. Potassium is the nutrient thought to be most related to the maturity of plants and it can, to some extent, make up for a lack of sun.

Other container-grown, spring-flowering bulbs, such as daffodils and hyacinths, can be treated in the same way until they die down; details of the frequency and quantity of fertilizer applications will be given by the manufacturer.

Mulching

A layer of rotted organic matter about 1-2.5cm (½-1in) thick on the soil surface round such plants as annuals and herbaceous perennials, especially peonies and hellebores, will do much to prevent water being lost from the soil when the hot weather comes. If the soil is dry, do not put the mulch on, as it will simply do a good job of keeping the soil dry; wait until the rains come, or water heavily with the hose before mulching.

Lawn care

During normal weather conditions in temperate climates, the grass on lawns will need cutting every seven to ten days and every five days if the grass mixture is a really fine one and the turf of bowling-green texture.

If the grass is cut less often, much greater length of grass blade is removed from each grass plant per mowing. The fine grasses do not respond well to this occasional severe cutting, with the result that the coarse grasses have less to compete with and so flourish. The end product is a lawn consisting mainly of rye grass, annual meadow grass, creeping bent, even couch and an increasing proportion of weeds and moss.

Cutting very frequently, on the other hand, weakens the coarse grasses and encourages the finer ones. Since much of the mixture which provides a fine lawn consists of sheep's fescue, this is not surprising; the fescue originates on hills and downs cropped continuously by sheep, rabbits and other grazing animals, so that over the centuries these grasses have developed constitutions which ensure their survival in the face of such attacks.

A good height at which to keep the grass is 1cm (½in) if it is really fine, otherwise 2cm (¾in) will be short enough. The best finish will be obtained with a mower which has about 8-10 blades on the cutting cylinder. The current view on removing grass cuttings is that mowing should be done with a collecting box or bag attached to the mower, otherwise the mowings lying on the lawn surface encourage worms, spread weeds and prevent aeration, but in dry weather they can be left to act as a minor mulch.

Many of the greenhouse fuchsias, like this one, are almost hardy. With only a little heat in the greenhouse, they will flower all through a mild winter.

Late spring is one of the best times to treat lawn weeds with a selective hormone weedkiller, since the weeds will be growing fast and the chemical will be rapidly absorbed and equally rapidly spread round the plant in the sap. Feeding the lawn in mid-spring will have encouraged growth in any case. Use the weedkiller evenly, whether in solid or liquid form; in general, apply it about two days after the last cut, and leave two or three days at least before the next cut. Hormone weedkillers are extremely potent, and whether you are using a solution or powder form, it is essential to choose a calm, windless day for application (see Flower Garden Controls and Treatment section).

Shading

Sometime in late spring, the greenhouse should have shading applied to it, especially if it is a three-quarter span or lean-to against a south-facing wall. This is often chosen as an ideal situation for a greenhouse and certainly it protects from north winds and obtains the maximum effect from the sun's heat. But it can get extremely hot and glaringly light, conditions in which only cacti are happy.

Shading is essential; hessian, chain laths, plastic sheet or Venetian blinds all provide temporary shading which can be made automatic, depending on the light conditions, or you can put a wash on the glass. An easily made, inexpensive one consists of a mixture of quicklime or fresh hydrated lime and sufficient water to give it the consistency of milk; adding a little size to the mixture helps it to stick. There are proprietary washes as well; one of these becomes transparent when rained on but remains opaque in sunny weather and also, unfortunately in dull, dry weather.

Weeding

Weeding amongst small plants is vital if you want a good display of bedding and annual plants, from mid-summer until autumn. The biennials in the nursery bed should be carefully watched, too, and perennial weeds in borders amongst herbaceous perennials should be systematically eradicated while still tiny, otherwise you will never be rid of such unwelcome plants as ground-elder, bindweed and oxalis. The hoe and the handfork are great allies for cultivated ground; paths, drives, paved terraces, patios, garage aprons and steps can be kept clear with chemical weedkillers (see Flower Garden Controls and Treatment section).

Compost-heap making

The material for this will mainly be lawn-mowings, which are excellent as they heat up quickly, weeds, and cut-back spring-flowering plants. There may also be some excess plant growth in the pool, which will need clearing out, and there are bound to be leaves, which seem to come down whatever the time of the year. As you make the heap, alternate layers of vegetative material with activator or sulphate of ammonia or, better still, with a thin layer of animal manure.

Watering

Unless the weather is unseasonably hot, watering will be confined to the greenhouse plants and will be a daily necessity. Water which is at the same temperature as the atmosphere is best, so there should be a tank containing it in the greenhouse. A galvanized iron one, covered so that light is completely excluded, will ensure that the water remains clean and free from algae, dirt, insects, disease and even small mammals. A water-butt outdoors to collect drainpipe overflows should also be covered, but it is difficult to keep the water clean in these. A strainer on the end of the pipe will help but may result in flooding unless cleared out regularly. Butts made of polythene or plastic tend to encourage the growth of algae internally. The same is true of watering-cans; galvanized or painted ones are best.

Ventilating

Roof ventilators in the greenhouse can be left open permanently; side ventilators can often be opened during the day and on really hot days doors can be left open. The temperature can also be lowered by damping down, that is, sprinkling the floor, staging, walls and plants with water two or three times a day.

Frames must be ventilated, too; this is very important, as they will contain various young plants which will be wanted for planting out at the end of late spring or early summer. On warm, sunny days, the lights can be pushed back completely and as the night temperature rises, they can be propped open at night, gradually being lifted more and more until they are left off altogether, unless the temperature is still dropping below 10°C (50°F) at night.

Treating pests and diseases

Greenfly and caterpillars will be the main problems but another pest which will become an unseen nuisance from now on is the capsid. This is a green insect which feeds by sucking the sap from young leaves and shoot tips and from flower buds, with the result that the flowers, if they develop at all, are misshapen, lopsided and stunted. Dahlias and chrysanthemums are particularly vulnerable.

Capsids are about ten times larger than greenfly and quick-moving; they drop to the ground when disturbed, so are often missed. Damaged leaves will have pin-prick holes to start with, but rapidly become tattered and new shoot growth stops. This is one case when precautionary spraying is advisable, before damage or pests are seen, at the beginning of late spring and again as the manufacturers advise.

Another unseen pest which can do a lot of damage to narcissus bulbs is the narcissus bulb fly. The adults lay eggs in the soil close to the bulb's neck and the maggots which hatch bore into the bulb and feed in the centre for about two months from early summer onwards. Even if the bulbs do not die at once, the following year they will produce only a few short leaves. Dusting the soil round bulbs with an insecticide in the middle of late spring helps and should be repeated twice more at about two-week intervals.

Slugs and snails will need trapping or otherwise treating and there may be some grey mould in the greenhouse, which can be dealt with satisfactorily by hand removal (see Flower Garden Controls and Treatment section).

Plants in flower

Achillea, Aethionema, Alyssum, Anemone, Aquilegia, Arabis, Arenaria, Armeria, Convallaria Daisy, Dicentra, Erysimum alpinum, Euphorbia, Forget-me-not, Foxglove, Globe flower (trollius), London Pride (Saxifraga x urbium), Mimulus, Pansy, Primula rosea, Saxifraga (mossy), Tulip, Wallflower

Early Summer

Early summer can be one of the most attractive times of the year in the garden. Plant growth is at its lushest and freshest, leaves and flowers are clean, bright and not yet battered by summer thunderstorms and many of the herbaceous perennials are in full flower. They will provide the main display of colour but the hardy annuals will be coming along fast and will begin to make themselves obvious by the end of early summer.

Most of the initial work of sowing, planting, pricking out and thinning will have been done, but if you were rushed in spring, the remnants of these jobs will need to be cleared up. A final potting can be given to many greenhouse residents and thereafter this will only need to be done occasionally, unless you are into taking cuttings of everything in sight.

With a chance of really hot weather any time from now through the rest of the summer, watering will become one of the more important jobs, particularly in the greenhouse. A few days without rain on sandy soils and plants will become distressed, particularly the small ones and those just planted out. The temperature in the greenhouse will probably need lowering, rather than the reverse, and cuttings in frames should be allowed some ventilation, too.

There will be quite a lot of tidying-up jobs, such as deadheading, training, stopping and tying but some of these could be called hard work, though they are essential for good displays of flowers, whether first or second flushes. One heavy job which will need doing if you want to sow a lawn in autumn is cultivating the site, as a preliminary to fallowing it for the summer. You could leave it till autumn, but the weed crop is likely to be fairly heavy if you do and will appear at the same time as the new grass seedlings.

At~a~glance diary

Prepare the soil for: sowing seed and planting outdoors

Prepare compost for: sowing seed and potting under glass

Sow seeds outdoors of: Canterbury bells, double daisies, forget-me-not, foxglove hollyhock, mullein (Verbascum bombyciferum), primulas, polyanthus, primrose, sweet william, wallflower; herbaceous and alpine perennials, aquilegia, aubrieta, alyssum, armeria, delphinium, lupin, oriental poppy

Sow seeds under glass of: cineraria, calceolaria, Primula malacoides, P. obconica, P. sinensis, P. stellata

Plant outdoors: half-hardy annuals and bedding plants, dahlia

Prick out: cineraria, cobaea, ipomoea, Primula malacoides sown in late spring, other primulas sown in early summer if they have grown fast enough

Pot: late-flowering chrysanthemums, cineraria, cobaea, coleus, ipomoea, Primula malacoides; plants permanently in pots as required; rooted cuttings of fuchsia and pelargonium

Thin: hardy annuals, half-hardy annuals and bedding plants, biennials

Transplant: biennials sown in late spring

Feed: pot plants repotted in early and mid-spring, hippeastrum, spring-flowering bulbs if still growing, sweetpea, lawns on light soils

Stake: border carnations, freesias if not already done

Train, tie in: chrysanthemum, dahlia, delphinium, sweetpea, violet

Divide: auricula, iris (bearded), polyanthus, primrose

Weed: as necessary, including pools

Routine work: mow, deadhead, water, make compost heap ventilate and damp down greenhouse

Pests and diseases: caterpillars, capsid bug, flea beetle, greenfly, leaf miner, mealy bug, red spider mite, rust, whitefly

Jobs to do

Preparing the soil for sowing seed outdoors

With the summer season officially here, the main seed-sowing period is over and you may in fact have more than enough work on your hands without adding to it. However, through lack of time, some seeds that should have been sown in late spring may have been left out and there are plants which should be sown specifically in early summer. Soil can therefore be prepared in the usual way for sowing (see Early Spring) in the nursery bed.

Preparing compost for sowing seed under glass

Again there is little work to be done here, except to ensure a display next winter and spring and, if you do not have any seed compost left over from late spring, make up a new batch and cover it with black plastic sheet until needed.

Preparing the soil for planting outdoors

Planting may also be a case of catching up with late spring or of planting which has been delayed due to bad weather, but in any case, clear the site of weeds and rubbish, scatter a little compound fertilizer on the soil and fork it a few centimetres (inches) deep, about a week before planting.

You can also, with advantage, choose a site for a new lawn and start to prepare it now. Cultivate it by digging or with a rotavator to 23cm (9in) deep or to the depth of the topsoil and leave roughly broken up. You may find grey-brown caterpillars and bright-yellow 'worms' in it as you do so, especially if it is old turfland or meadow; these are leather-jackets (daddy-long-legs larvae) and wireworms which should be destroyed, though birds may do this for you as you work.

The ground can then be dressed with rotted organic matter at 2.5kg per sq m (5lb per sq yd), or coarse peat at 3kg per sq m (6lb per sq yd) and left fallow through the summer. This results in weed seeds germinating: these can be hoed off at intervals, each time a fresh infestation appears,

Achimenes are a delightful rhizomatous greenhouse plant, flowering for many weeks in summer.

until most of the weed-seed population on the site has been destroyed. You can alternatively use a 'new lawn' weed-killer at the time of grass germination, but the seedling weeds do provide compost-heap material. After hoeing, rake the soil to an even, smooth surface.

If you are dealing with a heavy soil, it is well worth while mixing in coarse sand as you cultivate, at a rate of 6kg per sq m (14lb per sq yd).

Preparing compost for indoor planting

From now until autumn, you should always have a supply of compost ready for potting, as plants permanently in pots may need re-potting and others grown from seed will need potting on at irregular intervals through the summer (see potting compost, Late Winter).

Sweet williams are one of the oldest cultivated flowers, dating from medieval times. They will self-sow regularly.

Sowing seed outdoors

Seeds to sow outside in early summer can be any of the biennials sown last month, though they will flower some weeks later next spring, and also forget-me-nots, but leave these until late in early summer. Primulas, polyanthus and primroses can be sown outdoors in a shady nursery bed.

There are also some herbaceous perennials which will grow easily from seed sown now, in a nursery bed, to be transplanted in early autumn to their permanent places. They include aquilegia, delphinium, hollyhock, lupin, oriental poppy and such rock plants as aubrieta and armeria. It is worth trying any seed you have available now from perennials and rock plants, as germination of fresh seed, sown as soon as ripe, is nearly always better than if left until the following spring. Plants from early and mid-summer sowings will then be strong enough and large enough to survive the winter weather.

Sowing seed under glass

Primula malacoides, sown in late spring, may also be sown now, to flower late in winter and in early spring next year; *P. sinensis*, *P. stellata* and *P. obconica* can be sown now as well. Cineraria is another beautiful greenhouse plant for winter flowering which needs to be sown now, for flowering with the primulas. There are some glorious colours amongst modern cinerarias and you could fill a greenhouse with these plants alone. The range of colour covers pink, rose, white, purple, light and royal blue, crimson and bi-colours.

Calceolarias are also showy flowering pot-plants for early-summer sowing to bloom in early spring; the range of colour is quite different, covering shades of yellow and orange, bronze, scarlet and cerise, often heavily spotted with red or bronze. They provide a complete contrast in form, too, with petals fused to form a pouch, instead of the single rays of the daisy-like cinerarias. Calceolarias are a little more sensitive to low temperatures than cinerarias and should always be free from frosts, with a temperature in winter preferably between 7° and 10°C (45 and 50°F).

Planting outdoors

It should be perfectly safe by now to plant dahlias outdoors; if night frosts are still about, then the weather is very unseasonable and you will have to keep the plants in frames a little longer or cover them with cloches, if not too tall. Treat bedding plants the same way, provided they have been hardened off.

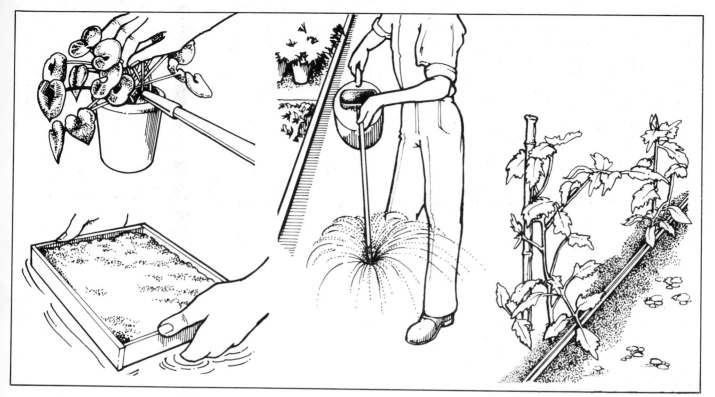

Pricking out

There will be little pricking out to do in the greenhouse. The cinerarias and *Primula malacoides* sown last month will probably be ready sometime this month to go into trays or, if you only have a few, into pans. Keep them as cool as possible and move them out into a cold frame, shaded from sun, as soon as they have recovered from pricking out. Cobaea and ipomoea should go into 9cm (3½in) pots unless you have sown them singly in 5cm (2in) peat pots, where they can stay until the roots begin to show through the sides or base.

Potting

Plants to go into their final pots and stand outside are the late-flowering chrysanthemums (see Late Spring). Fast-growing or vigorous plants permanently in pots, such as chlorophytum, cissus, jasmine, passion flower and tradescantia, will need re-potting. Seeds sown in late spring and pricked out at the end of that season may need individual pots in early summer, 5 or 7.5cm (2 or 3in) in diameter, depending on the size of the rootballs. These will be cinerarias and *Primula malacoides* and they can then go into a shaded cold frame. Cobaea, ipomoea and coleus will also need potting on; the size will depend on the size of the root-ball and this in turn depends on the time of sowing, or, in

Watering of plants needs to be done according to the type of plant and its needs. Spout watering from a can to the side of the pot prevents rotting of succulent stems—in cyclamen, for example; a seed-box is put into a shallow tray of water; a greenhouse is damped down to lessen the need for water; trickle watering supplies food as well.

the case of coleus, on the size of the plant when bought in late spring. Cobaea and ipomoea will both need quite large final pots, about 20cm (8in), while coleus do well in 12.5 or 15cm (5 or 6in) sizes. Fuchsia and pelargonium rooted cuttings will need larger pots, probably their final size (see potting, Late Spring).

Thinning

Any half-hardy annuals and bedding plants, hardy annuals and biennials you sowed in late spring outdoors will all need thinning this month; you will probably have to do two thinnings, one at the beginning and one at the end of early summer, depending on the weather and the time at which you sowed them. All the biennials but mullein will only need thinning once, because they will be transplanted before being put in their permanent positions. Mullein is sown where it is to flower, and will therefore be thinned twice, to a spacing of about 45cm (18in) each way.

Hardy Annuals

Name	Time of flowering; flower colour	Height and spread cm/in	Type of flower
Bartonia (Mentzelia)	mid–late summer; yellow	45–60 x 30cm (18–24 x 12in)	saucer
Chrysanthemum, annual*	mid-summer–mid-autumn; all colours but blue	45–60 x 22.5cm (18–24 x 9in)	daisy
Clarkia*	mid–late summer; pink, red, purple, white	45–60 x 30cm (18–24 x 12in)	carnation
Convolvulus, annual	mid–late summer; blue, rose, white, yellow	15 x 15cm (6 x 6in)	trumpet
Cornflower*	early–mid-summer; blue, pink, white	35–60 x 20–30cm (14–24 x 8–12in)	brush
Echium (viper's tongue)	summer; blue, purple, rose	20–30 x 25cm (8–12 x 10in)	bell
Eschscholzia*	summer; yellow, orange, rose, crimson, pink, white	12.5–30 x 12.5–20cm (5–12 x 5–8in)	poppy
Godetia*	mid–late summer; red, white, salmon	25–60 x 12–30cm (10–24 x 5–12in)	saucer, double
Larkspur*	summer; blue, rose, white	30–90 x 22.5cm (12–36 x 9in)	spike
Limnanthes*	spring–summer; yellow and white	15 x 15cm (6 x 6in)	saucer
Linaria (toadflax)	early summer–early autumn; crimson, pink, blue, violet, yellow	22.5–30 x 15–22.5cm (9–12 x 6–9in)	two-lipped
Love-in-a-mist (nigella)	summer; blue, pink, white	37.5–45 x 25cm (15–18 x 10in)	brush
Love-lies-bleeding (amaranthus)	early–late summer; crimson, green	75 x 37.5cm (30 x 15in)	tassel
Marigold*	mid-summer–early autumn; orange, yellow, mahogany	15–45 x 10–20cm (6–18 x 4–8in)	daisy
Mignonette	early–mid-summer; greenish, strongly fragrant	22.5–30 x 15–22.5cm (9–12 x 6–9in)	insignificant
Nasturtium (non-climbing)	mid-summer–autumn; yellow, orange, red, bronze, cream, crimson	15 x 10cm (6 x 4in)	trumpet
Phacelia	mid–late summer; deep blue	22.5–45 x 15–30cm (9–18 x 6–12in)	bell
Poppy, annual	summer–autumn; red, pink, white	45 x 20cm (18 x 8in)	saucer
Night-scented stock	mid–late summer; lilac-mauve	30 x 20cm (12 x 8in)	spike
Salvia horminum	mid-summer–early autumn; purple, pink, violet	60 x 22.5cm (24 x 9in)	coloured leaves
Sunflower	early–late summer; yellow	210–240 x 37.5–45cm) (84–96 x 15–18in)	daisy
Sweetpea*	early summer–autumn; all colours	210–240 x 15cm (84–96 x 6in)	pea
Sweet sultan (centaurea)	mid–late summer; purple, pink, yellow, white	45–60 x 20cm (18–24 x 18in)	brush
Viscaria*	summer; mauve, pink, blue, red, white	25–35 x 15–20cm (10–14 x 6–8in)	star

= can be sown in autumn to over-winter

Although it is generally thought that wallflowers do best if transplanted, they become much stronger plants if sown where they are to flower and thinned there twice. If this is done, the rows should be about 23cm (9in) apart and the plants thinned to a final spacing of 15cm (6in). Since they are part of the same family (*Cruciferae*) as the cabbage tribe, they should not be grown in acid soil, nor should they follow plants from that family, such as stocks.

Transplanting

At the end of early summer, the biennials may be ready for transplanting. If wallflowers are to be moved do it when

As well as being delicate and beautiful in colour and a graceful shape, freesias have an exquisite fragrance.

there are three true leaves present, and about the same size is right for the other biennials also. Wallflowers can then be planted 10cm (4in) apart in the rows, with 30cm (12in) between the rows, to make weeding easier. All these little plants need moving and replanting quickly, with as much of the root system intact as possible, from moist soil into moist soil, with a watering-in afterwards. Do the job in the evening, so that they do not have to contend with possibly hot midday summer sun before their roots have absorbed water from the new site.

Feeding

Pot-plants which were repotted in early and mid-spring will have used a good deal of the nutrient in the compost, and regular liquid feeding can start from now on, unless

they have grown so much that repotting or potting on is necessary. Hippeastrums should be fed, together with any other spring bulbs still growing. For really prizewinning sweetpeas, liquid feeding will do wonders, though with good trench preparation during winter, they may be growing so fast that extra feeding is unnecessary. Lawns growing on light soils will need a powder feed at half the normal rate, applied when the soil is moist and watered in; little and often is the guide to feeding turf on sandy or 'hot' soil. Cacti do not need feeding unless they were not repotted in the spring and then only once every four weeks or so.

The border peony, with its lovely colouring and full-blown flowers, is the personification of early summer.

Staking

Most plants that need staking will already have been secured but border carnations will develop their rather floppy and comparatively long flowering stems during the next few weeks. A little help in standing up will mean a better display but don't tie them rigidly to the supports right up to the buds, otherwise they will lose much of their charm. Stake freesias if not done already (see sowing, Mid-Spring).

Tying/training

Continue to tie in chrysanthemums, dahlias, delphiniums, lilies and sweetpeas as they grow and keep an eye on other tall-growing plants which may not be as sturdy as they look. Sweetpeas may begin to develop flowering stems towards the end of early summer in warm gardens; watch for the embryo flower buds at tips of the stems, otherwise you will be removing them automatically as sideshoots.

Early- and late-flowering varieties of chrysanthemums will need stopping; violets should be de-runnered, otherwise the parent plants flower less well. Take the runners off with as much stem as possible.

Dividing

Some plants – such as polyanthus, auriculas and primroses – can be increased by division in early summer. You will find that they have produced plantlets at the side of the parent crown; these can easily be split off with roots attached, replanted in a shady place until autumn and then planted where they are to flower.

Bearded irises can be lifted after flowering and divided every four or five years, otherwise they get crowded and flower badly. This is the time when they grow new roots, so dig them up, keep the new younger root or rhizome and throw away the old central crown. Replant so that the rhizome is only just below the soil surface; a little showing above the surface does no harm. Bonemeal mixed into the soil before planting at about 120g per sq m (4oz per sq yd) will help the roots.

Weeding

Continue to hoe or use weedkiller to keep weeds at bay. By now duckweed and blanket weed may be starting to grow in pools; duckweed is the tiny, light-green, one-leaved floating weed which collects in large groups on the water surface and blanket weed is the long, hair-like, dark green strands which grow submerged in the water. Chemical control in garden pools is not possible as cultivated plants will also be damaged, so frequent raking all through the growing season is necessary to keep these two water weeds under control. In pools well stocked with goldfish and freshwater winkles, the blanket weed will be eaten.

Routine work

Continue to mow the lawn, deadhead unless seed is required, water outdoors (do not forget freesias) and in the greenhouse and build the compost heap. Keep the greenhouse well ventilated and damped down.

Treating pests and diseases

Greenfly and capsid will continue to be a nuisance, various caterpillars will be about, including one rather beautiful velvety green kind which lives mostly on delphiniums, and Sawfly larvae feeding on the leaves of Solomon's Seal

Bearded irises can be increased by dividing the rhizomes after flowering, keeping the youngest end part for replanting, with leaves attached. Cordon sweetpeas are tied to a stake, and the side-shoots and tendrils removed as they grow.

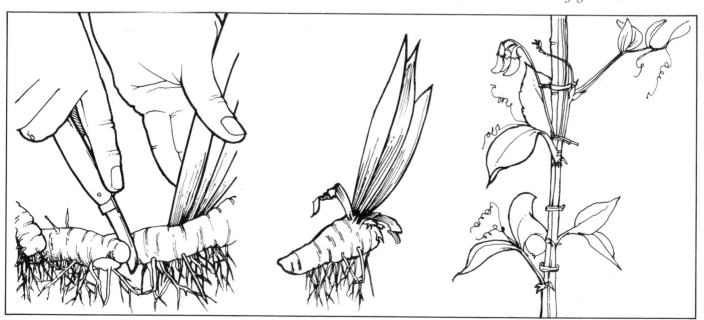

(*Polygonatum multiflorum*). A pernicious new pest is leaf-miner, which can do surprisingly bad damage, considering it is such a minute larva. The maggot hatches from eggs laid in the leaf tissue and feeds in the tissue, making winding, pale-coloured lines (tunnels) or pale-brown blisters as it moves about. Leaves can be so badly infested that they wither completely; chrysanthemums and cinerarias suffer badly. They will also be found on a variety of other plants but if the plants are growing in the ground they will not suffer so badly; it is the potted plants which seem to have little resistance. Remove affected leaves and destroy and spray the remainder with an insecticide.

Sometimes flea beetles attack seedling and young wall-flowers but an insecticidal dust applied as a precaution will solve this trouble; the symptoms of infestation are small round holes in the leaves and tiny, hopping, dark-coloured beetles. Whitefly, small white, moth-like creatures, can become terrible pests on greenhouse fuchsias, usually if the plants are kept too dry and hot. Likewise red spider mite

on most greenhouse plants; it feeds on the sap, mainly in the leaves, and makes webs. A hand lens will show the light red, round adults on the undersides of the leaves.

Damping down the greenhouse keeps it more or less free of pests as well as cooling it and making the air humid. Mealybug is another greenhouse dweller, partial to hippe-astrums but not averse to other potted plants. Blobs of white fluff on your plants are highly suspect and are likely to contain the bug, feeding on the sap.

Rust fungi can be a problem on such plants as hollyhocks and antirrhinums, pinks and carnations. Although they are not as widespread as the insects mentioned, they are very damaging where they do occur, resulting in early leaf-fall, and poor, stunted plants. Symptoms are raised, bright brownish-red spots on the under surface of leaves, easily missed until it is too late. Grow resistant varieties if available, avoid crowded conditions, and hand-pick diseased leaves, following with a fungicidal spray (see Flower Garden Controls and Treatments).

Plants in flower

Achillea millefolium, Alyssum, Antirrhinum, Annuals (hardy and half-hardy sown in early spring) Aquilegia, Arabis, Astilbe, Campanula, Carnation, Catmint (nepeta), Cerastium tomentosum (snow-in-summer), Chamomile, Daisy, Day lily (hemerocallis) Delphinium, Dicentra spectabilis, Erigeron, Euphorbia, Forget-me-not, Geranium, Gentiana acaulis, Geum, Gladioli, Globe flower (trollius), Helianthemum, Heuchera, Iris (in variety), Lamium maculatum, Lily (in variety), Lithospermum diffusum, Lobelia London pride (Saxifraga x urbium)

Plants in flower

Lupin, Pansy, Pelargonium, Peony, Phlox (dwarf), Pickerel (Pontederia cordata), Pink, Poppy, Primula (in variety), Pyrethrum, Red hot poker (kniphofia), Roseroot (Sedum roseum), Wild strawberry (Fragaria vesca), Solomon's Seal (Polygonatum multiflorum), Stonecrop (Sedum acre), Sweet william, Verbascum,

Greenhouse

Begonia, Cacti, Fuchsia, Ipomoea, Jasmine, Pelargonium, Streptocarpus (old plants)

Mid-Summer

Like early summer, this is a good season for a colourful display in gardens grown mainly for ornament. The herbaceous perennials will still be in flower and the annuals and bedding plants will really start to come into their own in the next few weeks, filling out their growth and covering the soil with a patchwork of brilliant colour. For a sheer display of dazzle, there is nothing to beat the hardy annuals when they are grown really well.

Your main concern will be to see that the plants have enough water; mid-summer can be the hottest, driest time of the year, only interrupted by thunderstorms, when the rain comes down so fast that the dry ground cannot absorb it and it runs away to the lowest point. Watering by hose, sprinkler or can will be necessary throughout the period and the lawn especially should be kept moist. Mulches put on earlier in the year will prove their worth now.

The greenhouse, too, will need much attention in the form of watering the plants and damping down; constant watering does of course wash the nutrients out of the composts before the roots can absorb them so you may have to increase the frequency of liquid feeds and repotting.

There will be a little planting and seed sowing, some thinning and transplanting and a general titivation of the displays in the form of deadheading and trimming. Some training will still be necessary and disbudding of dahlias and chrysanthemums to produce large blooms can start, but the work is not anything like the spring rush or the winter labour. Plant growth in general has reached its maximum and, as it will remain at this peak for some weeks, you can relax.

At~a~glance diary

Prepare the soil for: sowing seed and planting outdoors

Prepare compost for: potting under glass

Sow seeds outdoors of: pansy

Plant outdoors: colchicum, autumn-flowering crocus, Nerine bowdenii, seedling alpine and herbaceous perennials sown in early summer

Transplant: biennials, pansies if large enough

Prick out: cineraria, calceolaria, primulas malacoides, obconica, sinensis, stellata

Thin: hardy annuals, half-hardy annuals and bedding plants, biennials

Pot: calceolaria, cineraria, Nerine sarniensis, primulas malacoides, sinensis, stellata plants permanently in pots

Start: cyclamen (old tubers), freesia (from corms)

Lift: spring-flowering bulbs, biennials

Deadhead or trim: all plants and flowers that have died down

Disbud: early-flowering chrysanthemum, dahlia

Feed: greenhouse plants, cacti if not repotted in spring, sweetpeas, lawns in cool weather

Layer: sweetpea

Increase: border carnations from layers, bearded iris by division

Water: all as required

Weed: pansy seedlings, lawns in cool weather

Routine work: mow, build up compost heap, treat pests and diseases, ventilate and damp down in greenhouse

Jobs to do

Summer-flowering jasmine is hardy in sheltered places and its fragrant flowers will perfume the garden all summer.

Preparing the soil for sowing outdoors

This is only a case of preparing for one group of plants, which are to be transplanted, so a small seed-bed can be got ready in the nursery-bed; it will not be long in use (see Early Spring for details of preparation).

Preparing the soil for planting outdoors

Most of the planting now will be of autumn-flowering bulbs, so look for a place where the soil is naturally medium to well drained and on the sunny side. Mix in plenty of grit if it is not, about 3.5kg per sq m (7lb per sq yd), and a little rotted organic matter, if the soil is poor, at 1.5kg per sq m (3lb per sq yd). These bulbs are used, in their natural habitats, to very good drainage and baking sun in summer; you will find that most bulbs grown in such conditions, if you have them, will seed themselves without any encouragement.

Preparing compost for potting

Here the work to be done consists of potting on pricked-out plants from seed, so the compost should be the J.I. potting No. 1 type or whatever you are using as its equivalent (see Late Winter).

Sowing outdoors

This is an excellent time to sow pansies in order to have plants in flower from late spring onwards next year. If you have a heavy soil, the beginning of mid-summer is the most suitable time, and for warm gardens and sandy soil, the end of the period is preferable. The timing is fairly important: too soon and they will grow large enough to be badly damaged by wind and frost before flowering, too late and they will be so small when ready for planting that they will not establish before winter. Sow the seed thinly in rows about 20–25cm (8–10in) apart, making the drill about 2.5cm (1in) deep and just covering the seed firmly. If the soil is dry, water the rows before sowing, and sprinkle gently but thoroughly after the soil has been returned. Pansies need a well-drained soil.

Planting outdoors

Colchicum, autumn-flowering crocus and *Nerine bowdenii* can be planted in mid-summer; the depth of planting should be about 7.5–12.5cm (3–5in) for colchicum, 7.5cm (3in) for autumn-flowering crocus and sufficiently shallow for nerines for the neck of the bulb to be just above the soil surface. Both the crocus and the colchicum produce their flowers before the leaves at the end of late summer and in early autumn and will grow and flower best in a sunny place, though dappled shade is not unsuitable. *Nerine bowdenii*, from South Africa, will need sun and a wall to back the bed in which it is growing. Plant all these bulbs at a spacing of a few cm (in) from each other, and leave undisturbed for several years.

You can also plant outdoors in their permanent places the perennial seedlings produced last month; spacing will be roughly in proportion to the height of the plants, allowing a space between each plant of a kind, two-thirds of its height: e.g., aquilegias 30cm (12in) high would have 20cm (8in) between plants.

Transplanting

Any biennials sown in late spring which are to be transplanted should be moved now, in the way advised in that season and there may also be some from early summer, if they were sown early enough and have come on well. Pansies sown at the beginning of mid-summer may need transplanting at the end of it (see Late Summer for method).

Pricking out

Seed sown in the greenhouse in early summer will need moving into trays and will include cineraria, calceolaria, and *Primula malacoides*, *obconica*, *sinensis* and *stellata*. Done at the beginning of mid-summer, they may well need potting up separately by the end of it, especially the cinerarias and calceolarias. They can all go into the cold frame when pricked out.

Primulas, polyanthus and primroses, sown in early summer, will need pricking out 7.5cm (3in) apart each way, still in shaded places.

Thinning

There may still be some late-sown hardy annuals and half-hardy annuals and bedding plants that need a final thinning; early-summer-sown biennials will need one or two thinnings in mid-summer.

An herbaceous border, skilfully planted like this one, will provide brilliant colour from spring to autumn.

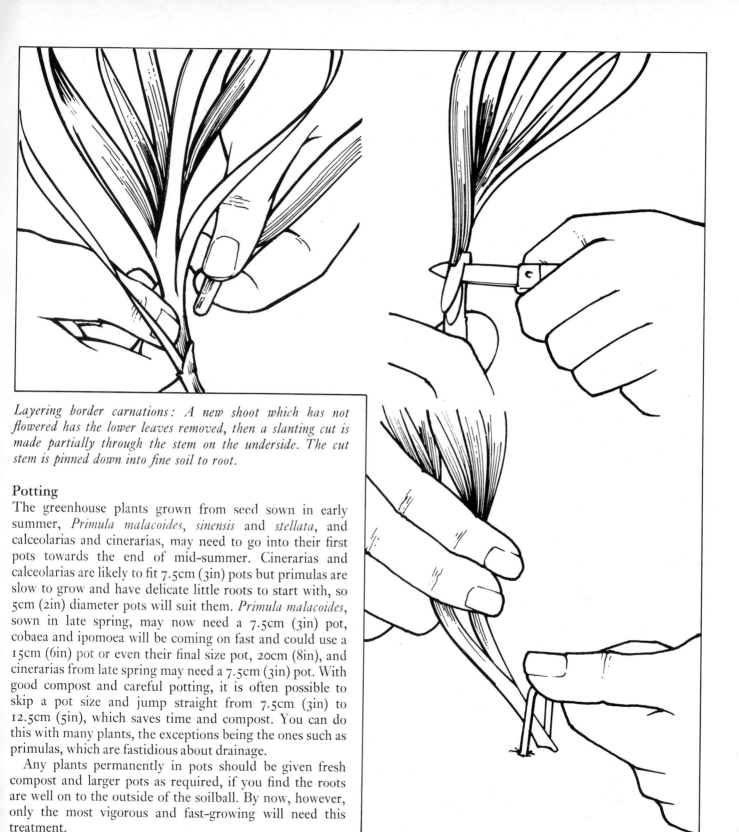

Layering border carnations: A new shoot which has not flowered has the lower leaves removed, then a slanting cut is made partially through the stem on the underside. The cut stem is pinned down into fine soil to root.

Potting

The greenhouse plants grown from seed sown in early summer, *Primula malacoides, sinensis* and *stellata*, and calceolarias and cinerarias, may need to go into their first pots towards the end of mid-summer. Cinerarias and calceolarias are likely to fit 7.5cm (3in) pots but primulas are slow to grow and have delicate little roots to start with, so 5cm (2in) diameter pots will suit them. *Primula malacoides*, sown in late spring, may now need a 7.5cm (3in) pot, cobaea and ipomoea will be coming on fast and could use a 15cm (6in) pot or even their final size pot, 20cm (8in), and cinerarias from late spring may need a 7.5cm (3in) pot. With good compost and careful potting, it is often possible to skip a pot size and jump straight from 7.5cm (3in) to 12.5cm (5in), which saves time and compost. You can do this with many plants, the exceptions being the ones such as primulas, which are fastidious about drainage.

Any plants permanently in pots should be given fresh compost and larger pots as required, if you find the roots are well on to the outside of the soilball. By now, however, only the most vigorous and fast-growing will need this treatment.

Nerine sarniensis, which is really not frost-hardy, unlike *N. bowdenii*, should be potted during mid-summer for flowering in early autumn; each bulb should have a 12.5cm (5in) pot and should just have its neck above the compost surface. A cactus compost would not come amiss, as they do like good drainage; after planting, give the bulb a good soak, let the superfluous water drain off and then give it a sunny position. The leaves will appear during or after flowering.

Starting
Freesia corms can be started off, in J.I. potting compost No. 3, planted with their own depth of compost above them. Put ten in a 20cm (8in) pot; they should begin to flower in early winter. Once potted, the freesias should be put outdoors in a cool, lightly shaded place and kept moist.

Cyclamen corms can also be potted to start them into growth for flowering in early winter; they are quite likely to start themselves off and produce new leaves from a completely dry corm sometime in mid-summer. Use J.I. potting compost No. 2, and a 12.5-15cm (5-6in) pot for most corms, though the really large old ones will need 20cm (8in) pots. Make sure the surface of the corm is above the compost.

The curious flowers of the passion-flower will set to produce egg-shaped fruit, orange in colour and edible.

Lifting
The spring-flowering bulbs that have died down completely can be lifted and cleaned if the ground is required for other plants; in any case it is better to lift tulips, otherwise they become weedy or flower badly, or mice eat them. Biennials which have finished flowering can also be dug up and consigned to the compost heap .You will probably have a bonus in the form of self-sown seedlings from some of them, so don't be too hasty to remove all the plant seedlings that appear; they may not be weeds.

Deadheading/trimming
Continue to remove flowers as they die, taking the stem off completely at the same time, as it is no use to the plant and will die in any case. Plants which will particularly need this attention are delphiniums, heuchera, iris, London pride, lupin, lythrum, monarda, pelargoniums, peony, poppy, pyrethrum and any annuals and bedding plants with flowers which have faded.

Catmint (nepeta) and *Campanula porscharskyana* will flower again in early autumn if the flowering stems are cut off and, in fact, they may already be producing good new growth. Rock plants which flower profusely on creeping growth will respond in the same way to similar treatment.

Disbudding

You can begin to disbud the early-flowering chrysanthemums now, if you want one large bloom on each sideshoot. It is likely that there is a miniature flower-bud showing at the tip of each shoot and other tiny growths in the axils of the leaves below it. These will also produce flowers if left to grow but should be snapped off without removing the leaves so that the plant's energy is concentrated on the top flower-bud. The smaller these shoots are when removed, the less shock it is to the plant. However, if you want sprays of flowers, do not disbud but leave them to grow. The plants will be at different stages of growth, depending on variety, so it is a question of doing the disbudding all through midsummer as they become ready, rather than all at once.

Dahlias can also be disbudded in the same way and for the same reasons; the more sideshoots you allow on a plant the smaller the flowers. Dahlias can carry more blooms of a reasonable size than chrysanthemums and less disbudding per stem is needed, usually only the removal of the two side-buds just below the top one. If each plant has many sideshoots the lower ones can be removed to good effect and the plant allowed to carry the remainder.

Feeding

Continue to liquid feed sweetpeas as in early summer and greenhouse plants where necessary, including hippeastrums; these may start to die down now and when they do, feeding should stop. Cacti not potted in spring may need one liquid feed in mid-summer. Lawns on sandy soils can have another half-strength powder feed, but not if the weather is hot and dry, because the grass is likely to be burnt. In these weather conditions it will not be growing much, so food is rather superfluous. Early autumn is the time when lawns should be given close attention, to put them in good condition for winter (see Lawn care, Early Autumn).

Layering

Sweetpeas that were planted in early spring can be layered now to prolong their lives, by detaching them all completely from their canes, laying the stems along the ground beside the row of canes and then training the stem up the fourth or fifth cane along from the original support. The last few plants can have the canes from the beginning of the row transferred to them. In this way, they will have another 60cm (24in) of cane to climb up and so produce more flowers.

Disbudding a chrysanthemum. Left: *The side buds round the top central bud are removed to leave the latter on its own.* Centre and right: *Saving home-grown seed. Cut the seedheads, hang up to dry, and roll and sieve to remove chaff.*

Increasing

Bearded irises can be divided if not already done (see Early Summer for details).

Border carnations can be layered and this is done as follows. Choose a new shoot which has not flowered, take off the leaves up to within about 10cm (4in) of the tip and then make a slanting cut just below a leaf joint, partially through the stem on the side which will be closest to the soil. Bend the stem until it touches the soil, pin it down with a bent wire just before the cut, and then gently pull the end of the stem more or less upright so that the cut is open and in contact with the sandy compost which you now put over and round the cut stem. The upright part of the stem can be attached to a small support. Rooting should occur within a few weeks.

Mid-summer is the time to take regal pelargonium cuttings, as they finish their flowering season now and new shoots suitable for cuttings will begin to lengthen (see Late Summer for method).

Watering

Give water where needed to all outdoor plants and in particular keep the lawn well supplied with water; using a sprinkler is best. Give sweetpeas a good soaking at intervals in dry weather. Water hippeastrums less and less as the leaves begin to wither but continue to water other greenhouse plants as they need it. Do not neglect your freesias in pots outdoors, nor any plants in frames, such as cinerarias or primulas; they will all need water. Cinerarias are very prone to wilt in hot sun and must have lots of water at these times.

Weeding

Little will be required, but pansy seedlings are easily swamped by weed seedlings germinating with them, so watch these right up until they need transplanting. Lawns can still be treated for weeds but preferably not in hot, dry weather; however, in such weather they are no more likely to be growing, with one exception, than the grass is. It is in cool damp summers that weeds cause most trouble and it is then that hormone weedkillers are most effective. The one exception is the yellow-flowered sucking clover, which spreads rapidly in hot weather and on sandy soils. As it is an annual, removal before flowering will do a great deal to prevent its appearance the following year. Hand removal is usually sufficient but a selective weedkiller can be used, if need be (see Flower Garden Controls and Treatment).

Routine work

Continue to mow (without the collecting box in dry conditions), make the compost heap and deal with pests and diseases as in early summer. Keep the greenhouse well damped down and ventilated.

Plants in flower

Agapanthus, Anemone (Japanese), Allium, Antirrhinum, Annuals (hardy and half-hardy sown in spring), Aquilegia, Campanula, Carnation, Centaurea, Chamomile, Daisy, Day lily (hemerocallis), Delphinium, Forget-me-not, Geranium, Geum, Gladioli, Gypsophila, Iris (English), Lily (in variety), Lobelia, Mimulus, Pansy, Pelargonium, Phlox (dwarf and tall)

Plants in flower

Poppy, Red hot poker (kniphofia) Rudbeckia, Scabious, Sweet william, Verbascum, Veronica, Water lily

Greenhouse

Achimenes, Begonia, Cacti, Campanula isophylla (Italian bellflower), Cobaea, Gloxinia, Hoya, Ipomoea, Jasmine, Passion flower, Pelargonium, Streptocarpus, Thunbergia

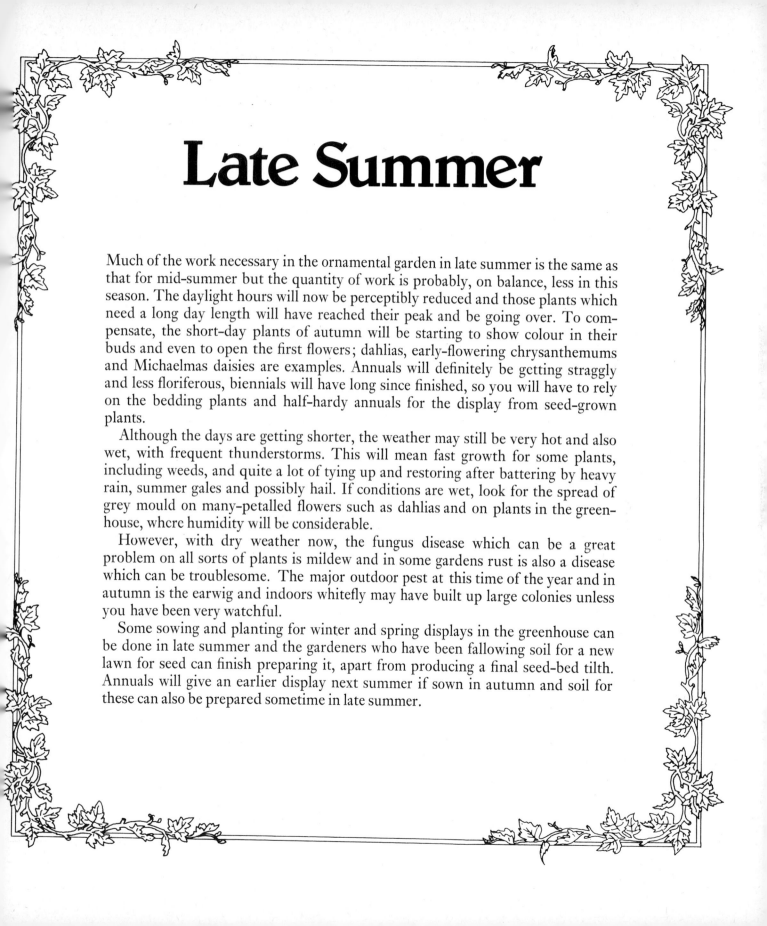

Late Summer

Much of the work necessary in the ornamental garden in late summer is the same as that for mid-summer but the quantity of work is probably, on balance, less in this season. The daylight hours will now be perceptibly reduced and those plants which need a long day length will have reached their peak and be going over. To compensate, the short-day plants of autumn will be starting to show colour in their buds and even to open the first flowers; dahlias, early-flowering chrysanthemums and Michaelmas daisies are examples. Annuals will definitely be getting straggly and less floriferous, biennials will have long since finished, so you will have to rely on the bedding plants and half-hardy annuals for the display from seed-grown plants.

Although the days are getting shorter, the weather may still be very hot and also wet, with frequent thunderstorms. This will mean fast growth for some plants, including weeds, and quite a lot of tying up and restoring after battering by heavy rain, summer gales and possibly hail. If conditions are wet, look for the spread of grey mould on many-petalled flowers such as dahlias and on plants in the greenhouse, where humidity will be considerable.

However, with dry weather now, the fungus disease which can be a great problem on all sorts of plants is mildew and in some gardens rust is also a disease which can be troublesome. The major outdoor pest at this time of the year and in autumn is the earwig and indoors whitefly may have built up large colonies unless you have been very watchful.

Some sowing and planting for winter and spring displays in the greenhouse can be done in late summer and the gardeners who have been fallowing soil for a new lawn for seed can finish preparing it, apart from producing a final seed-bed tilth. Annuals will give an earlier display next summer if sown in autumn and soil for these can also be prepared sometime in late summer.

At~a~glance diary

Prepare the soil for:	sowing seed outdoors in early autumn, planting outdoors
Prepare compost for:	sowing and potting under glass
Plant outdoors:	colchicum, autumn-flowering crocus Madonna lily
Sow seeds under glass of:	cyclamen, schizanthus
Pot:	calceolaria, border carnation (layered), cineraria, daffodil, freezia, hyacinth, Iris reticulata, lachenalia, narcissus, primulas malacoides, obconica, sinensis, stellata
Transplant:	pansy
Disbud:	early- and late-flowering chrysanthemums
Deadhead:	annuals, half-hardy annuals, pelargoniums
Feed:	chrysanthemums, greenhouse plants as needed, sweetpeas, lawns on light soils
Stake:	freesia
Rest:	hippeastrums
Increase:	pelargoniums from cuttings
Routine work:	mow, water, weed, build up compost heap
Pests and diseases:	capsids, caterpillars, earwigs, greenfly, leaf miner, mealy bug, mildew, red spider mite, rust, whitefly

Jobs to do

Above: *The Roman hyacinth is a slightly more tender variety of the common hyacinth, which was developed from it.*

Preparing the soil for sowing outdoors

If you would like to have annual flowers in bloom in late spring and early summer next year, early autumn is the time to sow them and you should therefore prepare the soil during the next few weeks. As they will flower where sown, you should choose a site which is reasonably sheltered from wind and cold, so that they survive the winter. Fork the soil to the depth of the tines and mix in an average-to-light dressing of organic matter, depending on whether the soil is mainly clay or sand, and remove all weeds and large stones as you go.

The site that has been left fallow for sowing a lawn in early autumn can now have lime mixed into it, if the soil is too acid, to bring it up to a pH of about 6.0-6.5. You can take the opportunity at the same time to break the soil up into a reasonably smooth texture, levelling it as you go and cleaning it of weeds and stones.

Preparing the soil for planting outdoors

There is little to do here; the same plants as were planted late in mid-summer can still be put in, so soil preparation will be as for that season.

Preparing compost for sowing seed and potting

You will need compost for both these jobs; the potting will include all sizes of plants and bulbs for Christmas flowering, which will do perfectly well in standard composts.

Planting outdoors

The plants to go in in late summer are the autumn-flowering bulbs but they should be planted as soon as possible, otherwise you will find that they are starting to sprout before being put into the ground. They include colchicum, autumn-flowering crocus, *Nerine bowdenii* and, although a few weeks earlier than other lilies, you can plant the Madonna lily *Lilium candidum*. It should be planted so that the bulb is only just covered with soil, preferably sitting on some silver sand, with a little more sand mixed into the soil round it. As with all lilies, be careful not to damage the fleshy roots. It will do best in slightly alkaline soil and a sunny place, though shade will not come amiss.

Sowing seed under glass

Seed of schizanthus and cyclamen can be sown in pans or seed trays filled with a standard seed compost. Schizanthus seed sown now, for flowering in spring, should be well

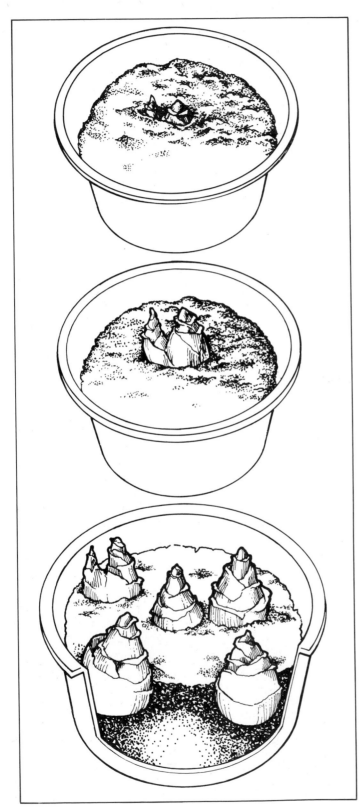

spaced out; it is important that the seedlings do not become drawn at any time, otherwise the adult plants will be leggy and will flower badly. The containers can be put in a frame outdoors, as schizanthus do not need great warmth for germination, but they should be covered until the seedlings do appear (see note on pricking-out, in Early Autumn).

Cyclamen should also be well spaced out, lightly covered with sieved compost and given a further covering of black plastic or glass and paper until they germinate. Keep the containers in the greenhouse; when sprouting starts, take off the coverings and put the seedlings in a shaded place, with a warm, even temperature. They will take several weeks to germinate and some seeds may take much longer.

Potting

Although it seems unnaturally early to be thinking about it, flowering plants at Christmas will only be obtained if you start potting them now. Towards the end of late summer it should be possible to buy bulbs, such as hyacinths, daffodils and narcissus, specially prepared for early flowering. You will get good results with these and be able to keep them for future flowering if you pot them in a good, standard compost rather than bulb fibre, which contains practically no nourishment.

Hyacinth bulbs are large, so one will be plenty for a 12.5cm (5in) pot; two narcissus or daffodil bulbs, with offsets, will be enough for the same size pot. You can put more into this size pot but it gets so crowded with roots that they come out of the drainage hole and up onto the compost surface. All these bulbs should be planted with the 'nose' (tip) of the bulb above the surface of the compost; don't make the compost too firm beneath the bulb and don't press the bulb down hard, otherwise the roots grow upwards rather than downwards.

After potting, put them in a cool place with a temperature no higher than 7°C (45°F), in complete darkness, and leave for about ten weeks, checking occasionally to see if they need water.

You can also pot the miniature iris, *I. reticulata*, for flowering early in mid-winter; use a compost slightly on the sandy side and cover the bulbs to their own depth, putting five in a 12.5cm (5in) pot. Lachenalias for mid-winter flowering can be planted in the same way now and both these and the iris can go into a cold frame until late autumn; water them occasionally if need be.

Bulbs for Christmas flowering need to be potted in late summer. Hyacinth bulbs should have just their tips showing, but daffodil bulbs should only be half-buried.

If cyclamen were slow to start in mid-summer, they can be potted now; the timing of various jobs with plants is never exact because it is dependent on the weather and can vary each way in every season. Nor is it too late to pot freesia corms; they will merely flower a few weeks later than if potted in mid-summer.

Calceolarias, cinerarias and primulas (*malacoides*, *obconica*, *sinensis* and *stellata*) sown in early summer, will now need moving into 7.5-10cm (3-4in) pots; those sown in late spring (cinerarias and *Primula malacoides*) will need moving into 10-12.5cm (4-5in) pots. Fuchsia cuttings from the spring will need 12.5-15cm (5-6in) pots, if they have not already been moved and regal pelargonium cuttings, taken in mid-summer, will have rooted and need individual pots sometime during the next few weeks. The size of the first pot will be about 7.5cm (3in) but if they grew sufficiently fast to need potting at the end of mid-summer, they may be ready for a second move into 11cm (4½in) pots by the end of late summer.

The carnation layers which were prepared in mid-summer should have rooted well by now and can be cut from the parent plant, carefully dug out of the soil and put into pots in a cold frame for the winter.

Campanula isophylla is not reliably hardy, but its prolific flowering ensures its place in the greenhouse or home.

Above: *In spite of its fragile beauty, the lily-of-the-valley is a tough ground-cover plant which can become invasive in a border.* Opposite: *Lilies rival roses in popularity; this is a hybrid called Imperial Crimson.*

Transplanting
Pansies can be removed to a nursery bed in the shade as soon as they are large enough to handle; lift them with great care and set them so that the leaves are only just above the surface of the soil. Doing this ensures short bushy plants, instead of straggly ones which can easily be beaten down by the rain.

Disbudding
The remainder of the early-flowering chrysanthemums can be disbudded (see Mid-Summer) and the late flowering varieties can be treated towards the end of late summer for flowering late in mid-autumn and onwards.

Deadheading
Continue to cut off dead flowers from annuals, bedding plants and pelargoniums to keep the displays of these plants as immaculate and brilliant as possible. Deadheading herbaceous perennials is not quite so important but you may be doing this in advance, in any case, by cutting the flowers for the house.

Feeding
Continue to liquid-feed all chrysanthemums in pots, sweet-peas if they are being so treated and greenhouse plants, as in mid-summer. The lawn that is growing on light soil can have one, half-strength feed early in late summer, but no later, otherwise it may grow too lush too late in the year and be 'soft' when winter comes.

Staking
Newly planted freesia corms should be staked now to support their long floppy leaves and stems later. Freesias growing from seed will nearly have finished their leaf growth, so will not need further training of foliage through the network of strings. Provided they have not been short of water during the summer, have been in a lightly shaded place and have not been subjected to too much warmth, they will begin to produce flowering stems in early autumn.

Resting
Most hippeastrums will come to the end of their growing season now and can be left completely without water; put the pots on their sides underneath the greenhouse staging. However, because modern hippeastrums are hybrids and have an evergreen ancestor in their family tree, those few in whom this influence is strong will not die down but will keep their leaves but, they should not be fed and should be kept just moist, so their metabolism slows down.

Increasing
You can take pelargonium cuttings at any time in late summer, the regals early and the zonals late. The regals have a much floppier habit of growth and fewer, but larger, trumpet-like flowers. The zonals have a dark band or zone on the leaves and heads of tightly clustered, small flowers; they are popularly known as 'geraniums'.

A shoot which will provide a good cutting will not have flowered or even have a flower-bud on it; the joints will be short, that is, the length of stem between the points where the leaves are attached will be 5 or 7.5cm (2 or 3in) long, rather than 10 or 12.5cm (4 or 5in). Lastly, the stem will not have started to harden but neither will it be soft

Bulbs, Corms and Tubers for the Garden

Name	Time of flowering; flower colour	Height cm/in	Position	Time to plant
Allium in variety	summer; purple, yellow, pink, lilac, rose	15–90cm (6–36in)	sun	autumn, spring
Anemone, florist's	mid-spring–mid-summer; red, purple, white, pink, blue-mauve	12.5–22.5cm (5–9in)	light shade	autumn, spring
Bluebell	mid–late spring; blue, white, lilac	30cm (12in)	light shade	early–mid-spring
Chionodoxa (glory of the snow)	early–mid-spring; blue	10–12.5cm (4–5in)	sun or shade	early–mid-spring
Colchicum autumnale (autumn crocus)	early–mid-spring; rosy lilac	20cm (8in)	sun or dappled sun	mid–late summer
Crinum x *powellii*	late summer–early autumn; pink	90cm (36in)	sun	mid-spring
Crocus	autumn, mid-winter–mid-spring; yellow, white, purple, lilac, blue-purple	7.5–12.5cm (3–5in)	sun	late summer, early–mid-autumn
Crown Imperial (*Fritillaria imperialis*)	late spring; orange, yellow	150cm (60in)	sun or shade	early–mid-autumn
Daffodil	early–late spring; yellow, white, orange, pink	15–60cm (6–24in)	sun or shade	early autumn
Dahlia	mid-summer–mid-autumn; yellow, orange, red, white, purple, pink, magenta	22.5–120cm (9–48in)	sun	late spring–early summer
Gladiolus	early summer–early autumn; red, pink, salmon, yellow, magenta, orange	45–120cm (18–48in)	sun	early–late spring
Grape hyacinth	mid–late spring; blue, white, violet	15–20cm (6–8in)	sun or shade	early–mid-autumn
Hyacinth	early–late spring; blue, pink, yellow, white, salmon, red; fragrant	20–25cm (8–10in)	sun or shade	early–mid-autumn
Hyacinth, treated	early–late winter; as above	20–25cm (8–14in)	sun or shade	late summer–early autumn
Iris reticulata	mid-winter–early spring; blue-purple, blue, violet; fragrant	15cm (6in)	sun	late summer–mid-autumn
Lily in variety	early–late summer; white, yellow, orange, purple, red, crimson, pink; some fragrant	30–210cm (12–84in)	shade or dappled sun	late summer–mid-autumn
Montbretia	late summer–early autumn; orange	30–45cm (12–18in)	sun	early–mid-spring
Narcissus	early–late spring; yellow, white, orange	15–45cm (6–18in)	sun or shade	early–mid-autumn
Narcissus, treated	early–mid-winter	15–45cm (6–18in)	sun or shade	late summer
Nerine bowdenii	early–mid-autumn; pink, salmon, white, scarlet	30–45cm (12–18in)	sun	mid-summer
Scilla	late winter–mid-spring; blue, white, lilac-blue	7.5cm–15cm (3–6in)	sun or shade	early–mid-autumn
Snowdrop	mid-winter–early spring; white	15cm (6in)	sun or shade	mid-spring
Tulip	early–late spring; red, yellow, orange, purple, white, pink, bronze, magenta	15–60cm (6–24in)	sun	mid–late autumn
Winter aconite	mid–late winter; yellow	7.5–10cm (3–4in)	shade	mid–late autumn

and sappy. You can also make cuttings of ivy-leaved and scented-leaved kinds now, though in fact they root so easily that any time in summer is suitable.

Make the cuttings about 11cm (4½in) long, cutting cleanly just below a leaf-joint and removing the lowest leaves. Put three or four round the edge of a 9cm (3½in) pot of sandy compost, cover with a clear plastic bag and put them in a cold frame outdoors, or in a shaded propagator, without the plastic bag, in the greenhouse. Watch their water needs.

Routine work

Mowing, watering, weeding and compost-heap-making continue to be necessary, but on a smaller scale than in mid-summer. Watering outdoors may not be necessary at all, in which case, weeding and mowing will be correspondingly much more demanding.

Treating pests and diseases

Capsids, leafminer, greenfly and caterpillars should be much less troublesome, though a last, precautionary spray against capsid and leafminer on chrysanthemum and dahlia and against leafminer on cinerarias is advisable. Continue to be on guard against whitefly, red spider mite and mealy bug under glass.

Earwigs will be the main problem, especially on dahlias, and there is still nothing much better than flowerpots filled with straw or paper and put upside down on top of the supporting stakes. Earwigs feed at night and hide during the day and such pots will be very convenient for them; check the traps daily and destroy any earwigs found.

Taking a pelargonium cutting. Left: *Use the top few centimetres (inches) of a new shoot. Lower leaves are removed and the cutting half-buried, at the side of the pot.*

Chemical sprays can be used but as the flowers have to be treated because they are the main targets, the sprays can do more damage than the insects.

A fungus disease that can spread rapidly during late summer is mildew; it infects many plants including Michaelmas daisies and chrysanthemums. There are varieties of both which are somewhat resistant to the disease. Mildew produces powdery white patches on leaves, stems and flower-buds sufficiently severely to kill leaves, malform flowers and stop the extension growth of stems. It appears during dry, warm weather and plants whose roots are short of water suffer heavy infections. Stuffy, badly ventilated conditions encourage its spread. Picking off affected leaves as soon as seen and spraying the remainder with a fungicide will help; alternatively, use a preventive systemic in advance.

Golden Dragon is an Olympic Hybrid lily, a stem-rooting kind which is not difficult to grow, given shade and moisture.

Plants in flower

Antirrhinum, Annuals (hardy, etc), Japanese anemone, Campanula poscharskyana, Catmint (nepeta), Chamomile, Chrysanthemum (including Korean types), Colchicum, Crinum, Crocus, Dahlia, Daisy, Day lily (hemerocallis), Gaillardia, Geranium, Gentiana sino-ornata, Geum, Gypsophila, Lobelia, Michaelmas daisy, Montbretia, Nerine, Pansy, Pelargonium, Phlox, Red hot poker (kniphofia), Rudbeckia, Scabious, Sedum spectabile, Violet, Hardy annuals and half-hardy annuals and bedding plants

Greenhouse

Achimenes, Begonia, Campanula isophylla (Italian bellflower), Cobaea, Fuchsia, Gloxinia, Ipomoea, Jasmine, Nerine sarniensis, Passion flower

Early Autumn

With the beginning of autumn there comes a quite definite change in the tempo of plant growth. As plants reached their peak in early and mid-summer, they ceased to develop and remained static but the often fresher, cooler weather of autumn seems to induce a kind of second spring. It is for this reason that most bulbs are planted now, annual and other kinds of seed are sown and herbaceous perennials planted or transplanted.

It is almost as though the sap starts to rise again and plants which flowered in late spring and summer often flower again now. Biennials which have been ticking over suddenly start to bush out and become leafy. Chrysanthemums and dahlias come into their full glory, and on established lawns the grass grows with renewed vigour. Even the birds revive and begin a minor dawn chorus again, to say nothing of their daytime chattering.

The more and earlier that you can take advantage of this regeneration, the stronger and better established your plants will be by the time winter arrives, so early autumn will be a busy season. In fact, there will be a good deal of work until the end of early winter, but it can be a particularly good time for garden work, with the soil in good condition and the weather mild. Lastly, there will be none of the great rush that occurs in spring when the sudden changes in the weather alone are enough to disturb the average gardener's blood pressure.

The grass will need a good deal of attention now, whether it is established lawn or a new one started from seed. The greenhouse can be cleared up after the spring and summer displays and made ready for the winter flowering plants, and weeds will also need more attention as they join the general regrowth pattern.

At~a~glance diary

Prepare the soil for: sowing seed and planting outdoors

Prepare compost for: sowing and potting under glass

Sow seeds outdoors of: some hardy annuals (see Table in Early Summer); lawn grasses

Plant outdoors: anemone, chionodoxa, crocus, Crown Imperial (Fritillaria imperialis), daffodil, grape hyacinth, Iris reticulata, Liliums auratum, bulbiferum croceum, davidii, formosanum, longiflorum, martagon, pardalinum, regale, speciosum, tigrinum, narcissus, scilla

Transplant: border carnation layers, pansy, polyanthus, primrose, primula

Prick out: cyclamen, schizanthus

Pot: calceolaria, cineraria, daffodil, hyacinth, Iris reticulata, lachenalia, narcissus, primula, rooted pelargonium cuttings

Lawn care: brush, feed, mow, rake, repair, topdress, spike,

Greenhouse: clean and disinfect, remove shading, move in all potted calceolaria, chrysanthemum, cineraria, freesia, pelargonium, primula

Increase: antirrhinum, pansy, pelargonium (zonal), viola from tip cuttings

Routine work: build compost heap, treat pests and fungal diseases, water, weed

Jobs to do

Preparing the soil for sowing seed outdoors
The soil can be prepared for sowing seed in beds and borders, in a nursery bed and on a site designated for a lawn. The preliminary digging and levelling where necessary should have been done in late summer, and now only the finishing touches need be applied early in autumn (see Early Spring for seed-bed preparation).

Preparing the soil for planting outdoors
Most of the plants to be put in now will be small ones; it is also the planting time for bulbs. The small plants will take more happily if the soil is reasonably crumb-like, moist but not soggy and contains a dressing of a phosphatic fertilizer, such as bonemeal, worked in two weeks in advance of planting. Use it at a rate of 90g per sq m (3oz per sq yd).

Bulbs do better with good drainage, though any reasonable soil will maintain a satisfactory display of flowers, given the same phosphatic dressing. However, lilies are more demanding and should have grit or coarse silver sand mixed into the soil to lighten it, for average-to-heavy soils. Single digging will be sufficient for all these (see digging, Late Autumn).

You can also begin to prepare beds and borders where herbaceous perennials are to be grown for the first time; this is a much bigger job, since the plants will be in for some years and cultivation needs to be thorough. Many perennials are deep rooting and double digging is advisable, mixing in rotted organic matter as you go. However, if the topsoil depth is shallow, one spit deep will be all that can be managed; be particularly careful to mix compost or manure with the soil in the bottom of the trench, as well as with the topsoil (see Late Autumn for details of double digging).

Preparing compost for sowing and potting under glass
Fortunately, there is correspondingly less work here, to compensate for the increase in outdoor work; there will be some sowing, a litting potting and some pricking out; you may have sufficient compost made up or bought.

The hardy herbaceous geraniums thrive in sun and rather poor soils. The one shown here, G. atlanticum, *is no exception and will be covered in flowers in summer.*

Sowing seed outdoors

Early autumn is a good time to sow sweetpeas, for flowering in early summer; if you plant them in the soil of the greenhouse in mid-winter, they should begin to flower in late spring, given enough artificial heat to keep the frost out.

They will be in their pots through the winter, but not growing very much, so J.I. potting compost No. 1 or its equivalent will provide the right quantity of food. Sweetpeas grow a long tap root and there is a type of disposable plastic cup which is just right for them, as it is long in proportion to its diameter. A drainage hole in the base, made by applying heat, is necessary.

Sow the seeds, one to a 5cm (2in) diameter container, covered with their own depth of compost. Some varieties are slow to germinate but can be encouraged to do so by making a little nick in the seed-coat with a knife. Put the pots in a closed cold frame and expect germination to start in about ten days' time; make sure mice cannot get at them.

The best time to sow is the middle of early autumn for the colder gardens but for the sheltered and warmer ones the end of early autumn or even the beginning of mid-autumn is preferable. After germination, take off the light but protect the seedlings from sparrows, as they nip off the young tips and leaves at a very early stage.

Quite a good choice of hardy annuals can be sown now, in their flowering positions, for flowering late next spring onwards; these include annual chrysanthemum, clarkia, cornflower, eschscholzia, godetia, larkspur, limnanthes, marigold (calendula), nigella (love-in-a-mist) and viscaria. These are all particularly hardy and, provided they are sown sometime during the first two weeks of this season, will be of a suitable size to withstand cold by the time winter comes.

Grass seed for new lawns can be sown (see Mid-Spring for details of sowing).

Planting outdoors

Autumn is the great season for planting spring-flowering bulbs and you can put in, the earlier the better, those listed for early-autumn planting in the table of bulbs given in Late Summer. Though none relishes organic matter, bonemeal or hoof and horn give them a good start, each mixed with the soil 10 days or so before planting at 90g per sq m (3oz per sq yd).

Lilies (except *Lilium candidum*) can also be planted in early or mid-autumn, giving them the same kind of soil treatment. An exception is *L. davidii*, which needs leaf-mould mixed into the soil before planting to flower at its best. The stem-rooting kinds, such as *Ll. auratum, bulbi-*

Right: *Dahlias are at their best in early autumn. This is Devil du Roi Albert, one of the most colourful decoratives. Below: For planting bulbs, a bulb planter can be used to remove a core of soil from turf, the bulb put into the resultant hole and the core replaced.*

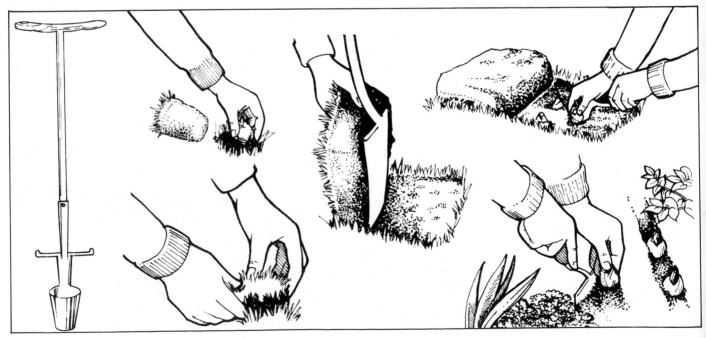

Narcissus February Gold, one of the cyclamineus group of daffodils and one of the earliest to flower.

ferum croceum, davidii, formosanum, longiflorum, regale, speciosum and *tigrinum*, should be planted 15cm (6in) deep; those that require acid soils are *Ll. auratum, formosanum, longiflorum, speciosum* and *tigrinum*, but *L. candidum* definitely needs a little lime. *L. martagon*, the purple turkscap, and *L. pardalinum*, the leopard lily, should be planted 10cm (4in) deep. Put them all in with a little silver sand beneath the bulb for perfect drainage.

Transplanting
Pansy seedlings put out in a nursery-bed in late summer can be transplanted in early autumn to their permanent flowering positions, whether a bed outdoors or a windowbox or trough on a balcony or patio. Use a trowel and lift them with plenty of soil to keep the roots as complete as possible; replant slightly deeper than their previous level, firm in well and water. Distance to plant apart outdoors is 22.5-30cm (9-12in), the latter in heavy soils, but in containers they can be spaced 15cm (6in) apart.

The primulas and polyanthus which were sown in early summer, can be planted where they are to flower, spacing them 15-23cm (6-9in) apart each way and planting in the way described for pansies.

If border carnations were not planted directly into the soil, they can be transplanted from their pots now into a sunny position where they are to flower.

Pricking out
The schizanthus sown in late summer will need pricking out. To keep them from growing thin and leggy, they should be moved as soon as large enough to handle. Put them 5cm (2in) apart in seed boxes. If the cyclamen have started to germinate, move them also when they have two leaves and a tiny tuber, and put them about 4cm (1½in) apart. Keep the temperature warm, especially at night towards the end of early autumn when the weather begins to cool off.

Potting
There is still time, early on this season, to pot bulbs for winter flowering, by the methods described in late summer. Also pot *colvillei* gladioli. For early-spring flowering, put five into a 15cm (6in) pot, and put them in the dark with the other bulbs. Cuttings of zonal pelargoniums rooted in late summer can be given individual 9cm (3½in) pots. Calceolarias, cinerarias and primulas sown in early summer will need pots 10-15cm (4-5in) in diameter at some time during this season.

Lawn care

Early autumn is a good time to repair, feed and topdress the established lawn, to get it into good condition for the winter. Bare patches can be forked up and re-seeded or cut out and replaced with turf; small bumps and hollows can be levelled out by cutting an H shape in the turf, rolling back the flaps and filling in or removing soil as needed.

Broken edges can be mended by cutting out a square of turf which includes the damaged edge, moving the turf forward and cutting off the broken part in line with the edge of the lawn. Fill in the gap behind it with soil and seed or more turf. (See details of turfing in Mid-Autumn.)

To maintain lawns in good health it is advisable to topdress them every autumn, but before doing this the lawn should be raked, brushed, mown and spiked. The topdressing can follow this treatment; put the mixture on in a dryish condition at 1-2kg per sq m (2-4lb per sq yd). Spread it evenly and work it in at once with the back of a rake or a stiff brush, otherwise it will have a smothering effect on the grass.

Autumn lawn treatment: Repair bare patches by cutting a square of turf and replacing it with good soil and grass seed. Topdress with a mixture of loam, peat and sand.

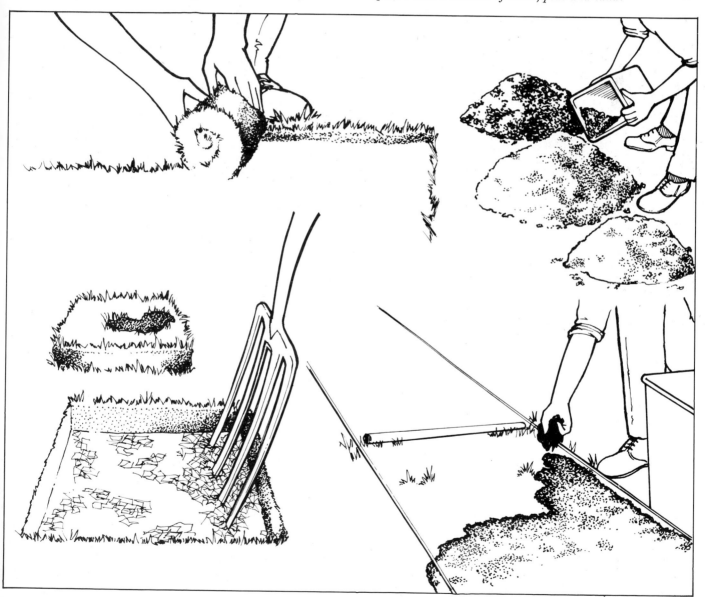

Gaillardia Goblin is one of the dwarf varieties, growing to 23cm (9in). It is a useful variety to grow as its short, sturdy stems need no staking.

The topdressing can contain loam, coarse sand and peat and for an average soil the proportions are about 6:3:1 but for heavy soils much more sand and much less loam are required and for sandy soils, much more peat, less sand and about the same quantity of loam are needed. Sometime during early autumn or at the beginning of mid-winter a fertilizer dressing can be given, either a proprietary autumn lawn feed, or a compound fertilizer, either of which contains much less nitrogen than the other two major plant foods. Too much in the way of nitrogen now will produce rapid, lush growth, which can be damaged by winter cold or badly infected by fungus diseases.

Greenhouse hygiene

As early autumn is the time to move plants which have been outdoors all summer into the protection of the greenhouse and as much of the summer display under glass will be nearly finished, empty the greenhouse now and give it a thorough clean. Do this while the weather is mild enough to stand any pot plants outdoors.

Move all plants, such as gloxinias, streptocarpus, foliage plants and potential winter-flowerers out and remove from the inside of the greenhouse all debris such as fallen leaves and flowers and compost spilled on staging and floors. Then scrub or wash down the whole of the inside with soapy water, or water with a mild disinfectant in it.

If there was trouble with pests or fungus diseases, use a diluted solution of formalin but wear rubber gloves and a mask if possible, as the vapour is irritating to eyes, nose and throat. Wait until all the smell has dispersed before returning the plants; this may mean leaving the greenhouse empty overnight, so choose mild weather for this, so that the plants can stand out at night without harm.

Clean any shading off the glazing and renew whitewash on the back wall if the greenhouse is a lean-to, so that the plants get as much reflected light as possible during winter.

Moving indoors
In the last week of this season, the late-flowering chrysanthemums can be housed; go over them for pests and diseases first, give them a good watering, make sure the ties are secure and put on a topdressing if the compost has got a bit low. Put them in the coolest part of the greenhouse and give them as much ventilation to start with as is consistent with the health of the other plants. Once the weather becomes changeable, ventilators need regulating from day to day.

All the freesias can go in; put them in a light place. Those grown from seed should be producing the first flowering stems by now. Cinerarias, calceolarias and primulas in a cold frame can be moved in as well but do make sure the cinerarias are free of greenfly and that leaf-miner is under control. Put them all in the least warm part, away from direct sunlight. If the weather is unseasonably warm, all can wait until mid-autumn before moving, as they are cool-temperature plants, and wilt quickly in warmth, especially cinerarias.

If fuchsias and pelargoniums in pots have been outdoors they can also be moved, depending on the weather. As soon as the night temperature drops appreciably, they are best given protection but this drop may not occur until mid-autumn.

Red-hot pokers more than justify their name : this bi-coloured hybrid is an interesting modern variation.

Planting Depths for Bulbs

Name	Depths cm/in
Allium	twice depth of bulb diameter
Anemone	7.5cm (3in)
Bluebell	10cm (4in)
Chionodoxa	7.5cm (3in)
Colchicum	7.5cm (3in)
Crinum	15cm (6in)
Crown Imperial	15cm (6in)
Crocus	5-7cm (2-3in)
Daffodil	10-15cm (4-6in)
Daffodil, miniatures	5-7.5cm (2-3in)
Dahlia	7.5cm (3in)
Gladiolus, large flowered	10cm (4in)
Gladiolus colvilei in pots	5cm (2in)
Grape hyacinth	5cm (2in)
Hyacinth	10cm (4in)
Iris reticulata	7.5cm (3in)
Montbretia	7.5cm (3in)
Narcissus	10cm (4in)
Nerine	surface with necks protruding
Scilla	5cm (2in)
Snowdrop	
Tulip	10cm (4in)
Winter aconite (eranthis)	5cm (2in)

Aquilegias grow wild in southern Europe. In gardens they are easily raised in sun or shade, in most soils.

Increasing

Zonal pelargonium cuttings can still be taken, early in the season; pansies and violas can be increased from soft tip cuttings, put to root in a cold frame and left there for the winter. Antirrhinums can also be increased in this way, if you wish to retain certain varieties.

Routine work

Continue to mow the lawn, build the compost heap, water plants in the greenhouse and weed; the need for water by greenhouse plants will decrease from now on. Weeding may increase, particularly in a wet autumn. Pest and disease treatment is similar to late summer but should also become less demanding, though whitefly and greenfly in the greenhouse can go on being a nuisance until well into winter if not dealt with very firmly.

Plants in flower

Anemone (Japanese), Antirrhinum, Annuals (hardy and half-hardy and bedding plants), Campanula poscharskyana, Catmint (nepeta), Centaurea, Chamomile, Chrysanthemum (including Korean types), Colchicum, Crinum, Crocus, Dahlia, Daisy, Day lily (hemerocallis), Gaillardia, Geranium, Gentiana sino-ornata, Geum, Golden rod (solidago) Gypsophila, Hosta (plantain lily) Lobelia, Michaelmas daisy

Plants in flower

Montbretia, Nerine, Pansy, Pelargonium, Phlox, Red hot poker (kniphofia), Rudbeckia, Scabious, Sedum spectabile, Spiderwort (tradescantia), Veronica, Violet

Greenhouse

Achimenes, Begonia, Campanula isophylla (Italian bell flower). Cobaea, Fuchsia, Gloxina, Ipomoea, Jasmine, Nerine sarniensis, Passion flower, Pelargonium (zonal), Streptocarpus, Thunbergia

Mid~Autumn

By the time mid-autumn comes, in temperate climates, most of the plant growth for the spring and summer is finished and it is time to clear the garden up and make it ready for the winter. Summer bedding displays will be over, the last of the early-flowering chrysanthemums will have been picked and the first frosts blacken the dahlias and remind us that winter is only a few weeks away.

Protection needs to be given as soon as possible to the slightly tender plants that have been outdoors in pots all summer. Heat will be needed at night in the greenhouse and occasionally during the day towards the end of mid-autumn, earlier in the colder and more northern gardens. Plants in the greenhouse have been watered a good deal during the summer but now will gradually cease to extend their growth, so the job of providing them with moisture will be much less demanding.

Before last month's false-spring growth comes to an end, some mulching and feeding of permanent plants and those intended for spring displays can be done; if encouraged to build up larger crowns in a last spurt before winter, they will come through the cold weather much better, flower earlier and more profusely.

Another clearing-up job that will start towards the end of mid-winter is leaf removal from lawns, paths and drives but in borders and beds, where there are herbaceous perennials and bulbs planted, the leaves can be a very good protective mulch. For annuals and biennials, however, they should be removed, otherwise such small plants will be smothered.

The lawn is another major area which will not require much work, as grass growth slows down markedly; there is still just time to make a new lawn from seed and if you are planning to make one from turf, the soil for this can be prepared now, ready for turfing in late autumn.

At~a~glance diary

Prepare the soil for:	sowing seed and planting outdoors
Prepare compost for:	sowing and potting under glass
Sow seeds outdoors of:	some hardy annuals (see Table in Early Summer); lawn grasses
Plant outdoors:	bulbs (as Early Autumn), also winter aconite and tulip; herbaceous perennials in well-drained soils; biennials Canterbury bell, double daisy, forget-me-not, foxglove, hollyhock, sweet william, verbascum, wallflower
Thin:	hardy annuals sown in early autumn
Pot:	calceolaria, cineraria, cyclamen, pelargonium, primulas, schizanthus
Move indoors:	all potted calceolaria, late-flowering chrysanthemums, cineraria, freesia, fuchsia, pelargonium, primulas
Clear up, cut back:	hardy annuals, half-hardy annuals and bedding plants, herbaceous perennials, rock plants
Lift and shelter:	begonia, early-flowering chrysanthemum, dahlia, gladiolus, pelargonium
Stop:	sweetpea
Rest and store:	greenhouse-grown achimenes, begonia, dahlia, gladiolus, gloxinia, streptocarpus
Feed:	herbaceous perennials, permanently planted spring-flowering bulbs
Increase:	herbaceous perennials by division
Greenhouse:	decrease watering and ventilation, stop feeding and damping down, watch for grey mould
Routine work:	finish mowing and weeding by the end of mid-autumn, sweep up leaves, treat leather-jackets on lawns and under newly planted small plants

Jobs to do

The primrose-like flowers of the polyanthus, grown from un-named seed, show a marvellous range of jewel-like colours.

Preparing the soil for sowing seed outdoors
It will still be possible to sow seed in mid-autumn, though it should be done within the first week. Seed-beds will therefore need to be prepared; remember that any pre-seeding compound fertilizer or bonemeal to be used should be put on about a week in advance of sowing (see Early Spring for seed-bed preparation).

Preparing the soil for planting outdoors
By the time late autumn comes, it is really too late to expect herbaceous perennials to establish successfully before winter and the only planting that can be done will be a few bulbs. However, turf can be laid at that time, so the site should be dug over in mid-autumn and prepared as for grass seed, but not to the fine tilth required for seed.

Preparing compost
In the greenhouse some potting of various-sized plants will need to be done, so a supply of potting composts will be necessary. Seed composts will not be required until late winter.

Sowing seed outdoors
There is still just time to sow the hardiest of the annuals and sweetpeas, if done right at the beginning of mid-autumn; they include those suggested for early autumn. It is particularly important that the soil is in good condition

There are dahlias to suit all tastes, both in colour and form of flower. For exhibition they are classified into sections according to flower shape: this one—Lucky Fellow—is one of the cactus section.

when sowing seed now, so that the seed germinates quickly and the seedlings can get themselves well dug in against gales, rain and snow.

Grass seed can still be sown, but the successful establishment of a good lawn from seed sown now depends a great deal on the weather of the next few weeks. If the temperature drops suddenly after sowing, the seed will take most of mid-autumn to germinate, and the seedlings are then very late and grow slowly. If bad weather sets in during late autumn, the result may be large bare patches, interspersed with sparse, weakly-growing seedlings and a good deal of time, money and energy will have been wasted. It is probably best to sow at this time only if you live in a district that continues to be warm until well into late autumn.

Planting outdoors
Although planting the spring-flowering bulbs in early autumn produces earlier flowering and better plants than

planting now, such a planting will still give you a good display. In fact, mid-autumn is often regarded by many gardeners as the best time to plant bulbs but, if you dig up a bulb at the beginning of early autumn which has been left in the ground since the spring, you will find that it has already started to push out roots. New growth in the spring-flowering bulbs does start very early after the summer rest and they then go on growing underground all through the winter, except in extreme cold.

Put in the same bulbs as recommended for early autumn, with the addition of tulips and, towards the end of mid-autumn, winter aconites, which produce bright yellow flowers with frills of green in late winter. *Iris reticulata* planted now will not flower until early spring.

Herbaceous perennials can be planted in those gardens with a light, well-drained soil; newly planted perennials will not do well through the winter in a soil which tends to become waterlogged and may not establish at all. The same advice applies to rock plants and to perennials grown from seed sown in early and mid-summer; such small plants are more safely left in pots or nursery beds until spring and can be removed to shelter or otherwise protected if need be. However, lily-of-the-valley planted now should be successful, provided some grit is added to a heavy soil. It is relatively shallow-rooting, so should not suffer badly from heavy rain; plant it so that the roots are about 5–7.5cm (2–3in) deep, and the points of the crown just above the soil surface. A slightly shaded position is preferred.

The biennials which have been coming on in a nursery bed through the summer can now be planted in their flowering positions. If you are planting a whole bed of one kind, the following spacings will ensure good growth and a good display:

Thinning
Hardy annuals sown outdoors in early autumn will probably need careful thinning by now. You can take the opportunity to weed at the same time, if this has not already been done and clear off any leaves so that the plants are not smothered. As well as being suffocated, they may be eaten by slugs, snails, and other pests sheltering beneath the blanket provided by the leaves and weeds.

Potting
Plants to pot in the greenhouse include the schizanthus pricked out in early autumn, which can now be put into 5–9cm (2–3½in) pots, and the calceolarias, cinerarias and primulas sown in early summer, which will either need their final 15–17.5cm (6–7in) or a 12.5–15cm (5–6in) size. The late spring-sown cinerarias and *Primula malacoides* will probably be able to have their final move into 15–17.5cm (6–7in) pots, in which they will flower. Pelargoniums from cuttings may have grown well enough to need a larger, 10cm (4in) pot. Pricked-out cyclamen may have come on sufficiently to need their own pots but they are slower growing and should never be over-potted.

Moving indoors
If the weather has been mild, tender plants in containers are probably in a cold frame but they should definitely be taken under greenhouse cover sometime during the next few weeks. Included in this are all the plants mentioned in Early Autumn for housing.

Clearing up and cutting back
Hardy annuals, bedding plants and half-hardy annuals will have come to the end of their flowering and should be cleared off and put on the compost heap, leaving the ground ready for digging in late autumn. The aquatic plants will be dying back fast and their remains should be cleared out of the pool, together with leaves as they fall.

Herbaceous perennials and rock plants can be cleaned up by cutting off the flowering stems and leaves to crown level but it may be more sensible to leave them. Although it makes beds and borders look gaunt and untidy, the dead

Planting Distances

Name	Distance to plant
Canterbury bell	22.5cm (9in) each way
Double daisy	12.5cm (5in) each way
Forget-me-not	15cm (6in) each way
Foxglove	22.5cm (9in) each way
Hollyhock	37.5cm (15in) each way
Sweet William	22.5–30cm (9–12in) each way
Verbascum	45cm (18in) each way
Wallflower	15 × 22.5cm (6 × 9in) each way

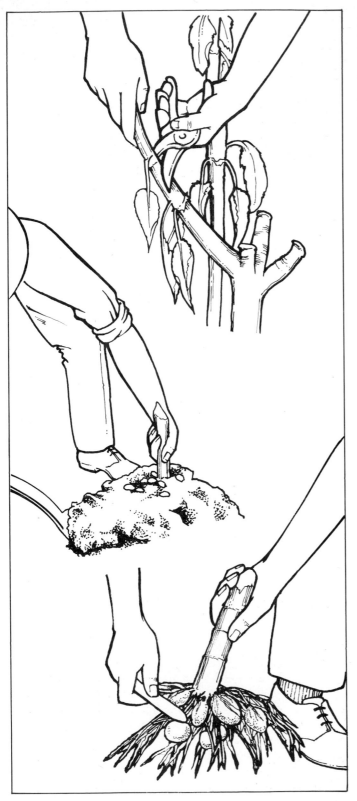

growth does provide protection from cold; this protection can just make the difference between life and death for some plants in a bad winter.

Lifting and putting into shelter

Dahlias can be left until the first frost, in mid or late autumn, but once their leaves and stems are black, the remains should be cut off, the tubers dug up and the soil shaken off. Tubers which are firm and uninjured can be stored in a frostproof place through the winter; they should be put into 7.5cm (3in) deep boxes, in the bottom of which is a layer of peat, dry leaves or straw. Peat or soil is then worked in between the plants after they are placed in the box, to cover the tubers. Dusting them with sulphur beforehand will prevent the spread of storage rots.

Keeping the storage material slightly moist prevents the tubers from wrinkling and if placed under the staging and kept at about 7°C (45°F), they will tick over until spring. In its native habitat, the dahlia is a perennial and sometimes, in temperate climates, tubers left in the ground all winter survive and flower the following season, though not as well as new plants grown from cuttings.

Pelargoniums which have been planted outdoors all summer should be cut down to leave about 10cm (4in) of their main stem, dug up and put into pots or boxes containing compost; it will do no harm if they are slightly cramped for root-room. The containers are then transferred to the greenhouse staging.

Early-flowering chrysanthemums, the last flowers of which should have been cut by the end of mid-autumn, are another plant to move into shelter. Cut the top growth down to leave about 10cm (4in) of stem and put the crowns, packed closely, into boxes of compost or fine loam. Then put the containers into a cold frame for the winter, closing it when frost is forecast.

Large-flowered begonia tubers should be dug up and boxed, in peat, to go under the staging. Gladioli will have to be taken up, cleaned of any top growth and any small cormlets which have formed round the base, and put in single layers in seed trays in a dark frostproof place.

Stopping

Sweetpeas sown in early autumn will need stopping: break off the tip of the main shoot just above the third pair of leaves. If this leading tip is allowed to grow, the resultant

Preparing a dahlia for winter storage: Cut the stems right down after the first frost, dig up carefully and label before storing the tubers in a frostproof place.

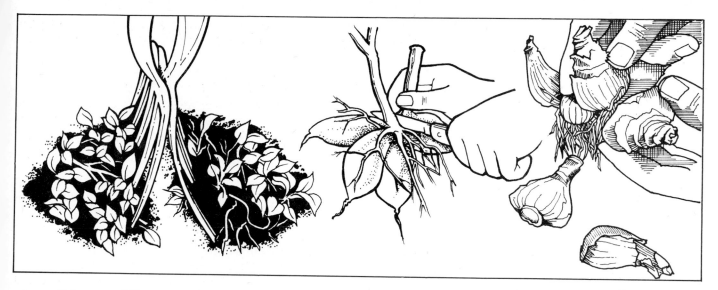

plant will be poor, if it ever reaches any length; its removal encourages two sideshoots to appear just below and these should be kept and used for training. They will need temporary support through the winter and any other sideshoots should be removed as soon as seen.

Sweeping up leaves

Towards the end of mid-autumn one of the biggest autumn clearing-up jobs will start, that of sweeping up and removing leaves. In some years the autumn gales will largely do the job for you but leaf removal from lawns is important because leaf cover, if left to lie, discolours the grass and weakens it.

Leaves stacked separately from the general compost heap, with a wire-netting surround, rot down into good organic matter within a year; sieved leafmould used to be an ingredient of potting composts, before peat became so easily available. Leathery leaves, such as those of evergreens, which are shed at times, take so long to decay they are not worth including; oak and chestnut make excellent leafmould.

Resting and storing

Summer-flowering tubers and corms in the greenhouse will be finishing their displays and as they do so, the dead and dying growth should be cut off and the containers put on their sides under the staging. There is no need to remove the tubers and corms from the compost; they can remain in it through the winter. *Nerine sarniensis* is the exception, as its leaves last through the winter; it should be watered occasionally, given a light place, kept free from frost and reasonably warm if possible. In spring it dies down and then rests through the summer.

Increasing plants by division: Divide herbaceous perennials with the help of two forks, cut dahlia tubers with 'eyes' attached, and separate offsets from the parent bulb.

Feeding

Established herbaceous borders can be supplied with bonemeal now to good effect, also permanent plantings of spring-flowering bulbs; apply 120g per sq m (4oz per sq yd), preferably when rain is due. There is no need to continue feeding late-flowering chrysanthemums; in fact, it can damage them if continued later than mid-autumn.

Increasing

This is a good time of the year to dig up herbaceous perennials and divide them. This job needs to be done about every four years, otherwise the plants flower less and less well. They should be taken up with as much root as possible intact; cut back very long ones to the main body of the root-ball. The plants are then divided, either by gently pulling them apart, by using a knife for solid crowns, or by using two forks, back to back. Replant the outside pieces and put the central parts on the compost heap or destroy.

Greenhouse work

Damping down should cease, feeding will not be necessary any longer and watering can be considerably decreased. Ventilators will need to be closed very much more at night if the temperature drops and for the daytime they will need regulating from day to day, as the weather will be changeable. Gentle artificial heat will be needed some nights and towards the end of mid-autumn is a good time to line the inside of the greenhouse glazing with clear plastic sheet to

A first-class herbaceous border, backed by immaculate hedges, takes a lot of beating as a garden feature.

retain warmth. It is now possible to obtain sheet on which moisture does not condense. Grey mould (botrytis) tends to spread rapidly in autumn, so be careful to remove fallen leaves and stems. Watch for the disease on the plants; flowers can be infected just as much as leaves can.

Routine work

Mowing will almost be unnecessary by the end of mid-autumn. The compost heap will be finished and can have a roof put above it to keep the worst of the winter wet off, weeding will be more or less at an end and pest and disease treatment will no longer be required, except for leather-jackets on lawns.

These grey-brown caterpillars are the larvae of the cranefly (daddy-long-legs); they hatch from eggs laid earlier in autumn in the soil and then feed on the roots of grass and also small plants. When adult they are about 2.5cm (1in) but the small caterpillars can do a lot of damage, feeding in groups in autumn and through the winter in mild weather; infested grass turns pale brown and dies, in roundish patches. Starlings digging into the turf are often a sign of their presence; watering it heavily, then covering overnight, brings some of them to the surface, where they can be collected and destroyed the following day (see Flower Garden Controls and Treatments for chemical insecticides).

Plants in flower

Japanese anemone, Catmint (nepeta)
Korean chrysanthemums
Colchicum (Autumn crocus)
Dahlia, Daisy, Gaillardia,
Gentiana sino-ornata
Golden rod, Michaelmas daisy,
Nerine bowdenii, Sedum spectabile,
Violet Begonia, Campanula
isophylla (Italian bellflower)
Chrysanthemum, Cobaea,
Freesia, Passion flower,
Pelargonium (zonal),
Streptocarpus, Thunbergia.

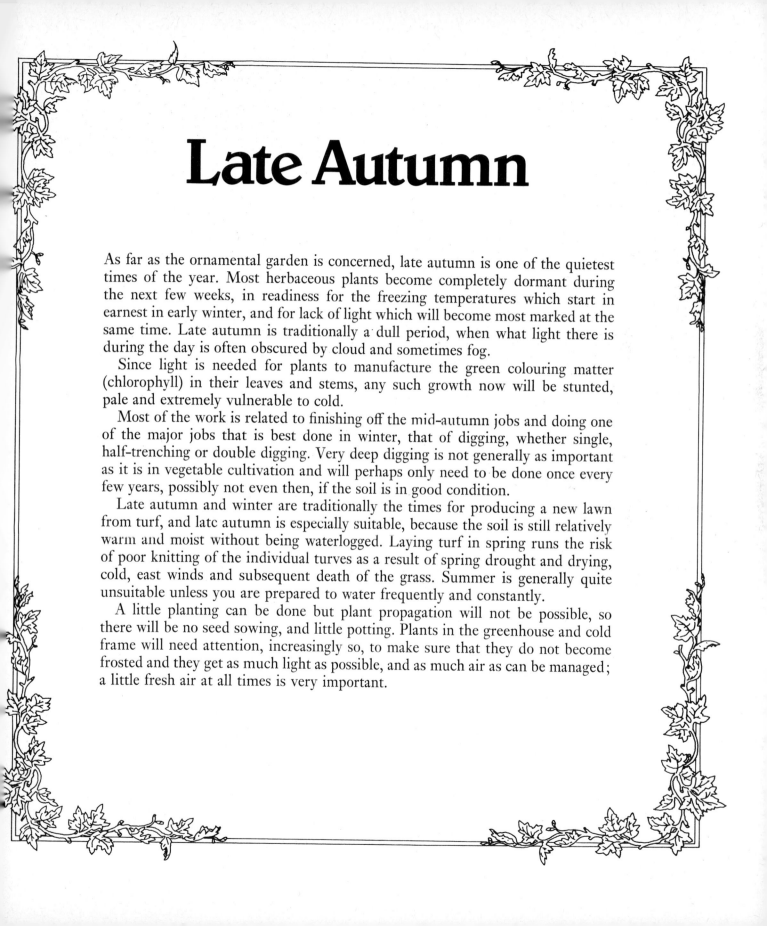

Late Autumn

As far as the ornamental garden is concerned, late autumn is one of the quietest times of the year. Most herbaceous plants become completely dormant during the next few weeks, in readiness for the freezing temperatures which start in earnest in early winter, and for lack of light which will become most marked at the same time. Late autumn is traditionally a dull period, when what light there is during the day is often obscured by cloud and sometimes fog.

Since light is needed for plants to manufacture the green colouring matter (chlorophyll) in their leaves and stems, any such growth now will be stunted, pale and extremely vulnerable to cold.

Most of the work is related to finishing off the mid-autumn jobs and doing one of the major jobs that is best done in winter, that of digging, whether single, half-trenching or double digging. Very deep digging is not generally as important as it is in vegetable cultivation and will perhaps only need to be done once every few years, possibly not even then, if the soil is in good condition.

Late autumn and winter are traditionally the times for producing a new lawn from turf, and late autumn is especially suitable, because the soil is still relatively warm and moist without being waterlogged. Laying turf in spring runs the risk of poor knitting of the individual turves as a result of spring drought and drying, cold, east winds and subsequent death of the grass. Summer is generally quite unsuitable unless you are prepared to water frequently and constantly.

A little planting can be done but plant propagation will not be possible, so there will be no seed sowing, and little potting. Plants in the greenhouse and cold frame will need attention, increasingly so, to make sure that they do not become frosted and they get as much light as possible, and as much air as can be managed; a little fresh air at all times is very important.

At-a-glance diary

Dig: all sites where perennials, plants from seed, bulbs and sweetpeas are to be grown

Prepare the soil for: planting outdoors

Plant outdoors: winter aconites, tulips, spring-flowering bulbs for late flowering

Turf: new lawn

Mow: established lawns, new lawns lightly

Stop: sweetpea seedlings

Protect: woolly- and grey-leaved rock plants, Christmas rose (Helleborus niger), agapanthus, red hot poker (kniphofia)

Light: Christmas-flowering bulbs

Cut down: greenhouse chrysanthemums as they finish flowering

Greenhouse: heat, clean glazing, ventilate, water and watch for pests and diseases

Jobs to do

The autumn-flowering colchicum, sometimes called autumn crocus, only produces leaves when the flowers have died down.

Digging

Beds and borders in which the small, temporary plants are to be grown do not require tremendous excavations; provided the humus and nutrients are renewed in them every year, they need only be dug to the depth of a spade (spit), rotted organic matter being mixed into them at the same time. You can spread this on the surface first, or mix it in with a fork after the main digging has been done.

Loamy soils, which already have a good structure, drain well and contain nutrients easily available to the plant's roots, need only have a moderate dressing applied, about 2.5kg per sq m (5lb per sq yd). Those which are on the heavy side and contain clay, making them sticky when wet and concrete-like when dry, may need about 3.5kg (7lb) for the same area, but if you find plants become very leafy and large as a result, reduce the application in the following years to 2.5kg per sq m (5lb per sq yd), or less (a light dressing). Soils which contain sand, shale, pebbles, shingle or chalk in appreciable quantities will need at least 5kg per sq m (10lb per sq yd), in other words a heavy application. Even so, they should have mulches of organic matter given to the plants all through the growing season.

Organic matter consists of the remains of vegetable or animal organisms, rotted down into a dark-brown, moist, crumbly material without smell. Though farm manure is excellent, it is difficult to obtain, but a good substitute is compost made in the garden. Other materials to use are leafmould, rotted straw, spent mushroom compost, seaweed, poultry deep litter, treated sewage sludge, spent hops, or peat. Treated sewage sludge can be obtained from local councils, who should provide an analysis of the nutrient content; you should also find out what the heavy metal content is, otherwise you may unwittingly be building up toxic amounts of copper, zinc and other metals contained in sewage sludge, in the soil.

Single digging should also be sufficient if you are planning to plant bulbs. Remember that they generally do best in light soil, so work coarse sand or grit into heavy soils at the same time, at up to 3.5kg per sq m (7lb per sq yd).

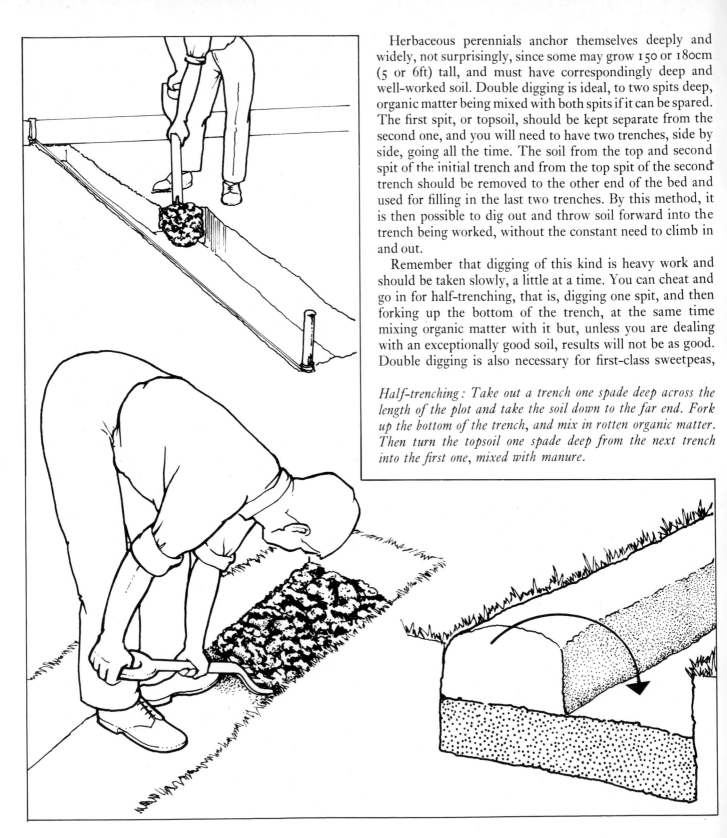

Herbaceous perennials anchor themselves deeply and widely, not surprisingly, since some may grow 150 or 180cm (5 or 6ft) tall, and must have correspondingly deep and well-worked soil. Double digging is ideal, to two spits deep, organic matter being mixed with both spits if it can be spared. The first spit, or topsoil, should be kept separate from the second one, and you will need to have two trenches, side by side, going all the time. The soil from the top and second spit of the initial trench and from the top spit of the second trench should be removed to the other end of the bed and used for filling in the last two trenches. By this method, it is then possible to dig out and throw soil forward into the trench being worked, without the constant need to climb in and out.

Remember that digging of this kind is heavy work and should be taken slowly, a little at a time. You can cheat and go in for half-trenching, that is, digging one spit, and then forking up the bottom of the trench, at the same time mixing organic matter with it but, unless you are dealing with an exceptionally good soil, results will not be as good. Double digging is also necessary for first-class sweetpeas,

Half-trenching: Take out a trench one spade deep across the length of the plot and take the soil down to the far end. Fork up the bottom of the trench, and mix in rotten organic matter. Then turn the topsoil one spade deep from the next trench into the first one, mixed with manure.

The Siberian wallflower, Cheiranthus allioni, *is a perennial species that does well in a sunny place.*

as they are strong, fast-growing plants with a large root system; even with the modern bushy sweetpeas you will get more flowers and brighter colours with thorough cultivation of this kind.

If you are fortunate enough to own a rotavator, this can be used, but unless it is one of the bigger, market-garden-type models, the tines will only penetrate about 22.5cm (9in) deep. Repeated use each year will result in the formation of a 'pan', a compacted internal surface just below the limit of the tine penetration, which will have to be dug or forked at some time.

Once the digging or cultivation has been finished, the soil can be left through the winter, even if it is still lumpy, because the action of rain, frost and snow will ensure that these lumps are easily knocked down into much smaller pieces by the use of a fork when spring comes.

Preparing the soil for planting
Some bulbs planted now will still flower at the right time next spring, so soil should be prepared accordingly, if not already done in mid-autumn (see Early Autumn for method).

Planting
Some experts advise that tulips should not be planted until the beginning of late autumn so, if you did not get them in earlier, little has been lost, even with the early spring-flowering species tulips. Winter aconites and other such bulbs as crocus, daffodils, narcissus and hyacinth will have a lot of catching up to do, so expect them to flower late from a planting of this date.

Turfing

Although growing a lawn from turf is said to be seven times more expensive than from seed, it does mean instant lawn, with none of the anxiety associated with nursing grass seedlings through attacks by birds, competition with weeds, drought, cold, waterlogging and leather-jacket damage. Provided you lay the turves correctly, in suitable weather conditions, the lawn will be established, to all intents and purposes, from the first two or three weeks.

Laying turf: Stand on a board, to prevent soil compaction, add or remove soil to adjust the level, and lay the turves staggered. Brush sand into the joins.

Turves are either 90 × 30cm (3ft × 1ft), or 30 × 30cm (1ft × 1ft); they should be about 4cm (1½in) thick, consisting of a uniform mixture of grasses, without weeds.

You will have prepared the soil in mid-autumn and now you need only apply and rake in superphosphate at about 30g per sq m (1oz per sq yd) a week or so before laying the turves. Choose a day when the soil is moist and the weather mild, with the possibility of rain to come, and lay the first line up and down the length of the site, starting at the edge. Put each turf down slightly looped, and gently tap it flat when the line next to it has been laid. This ensures a tight fit, as does knocking the edge of the second line against the first, and so on, as the work progresses. In order to get a

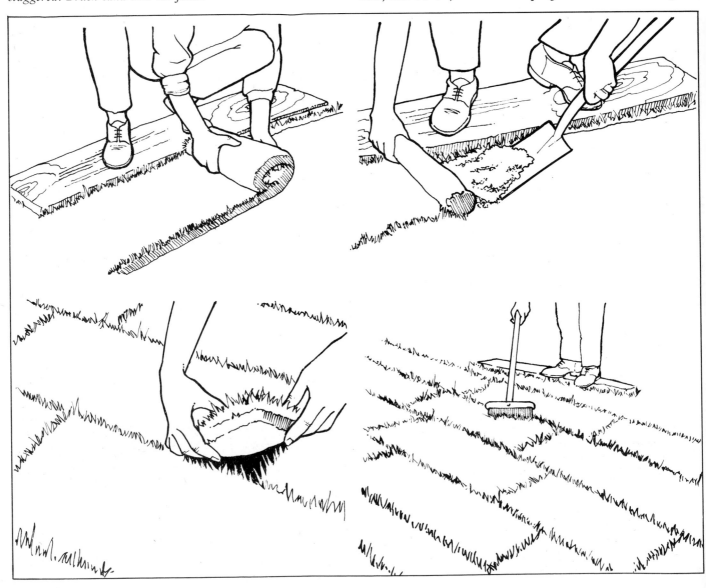

Biennials

Name	Time of flowering; flower colour	Height and spread cm/in	Sow	Transplant	Thin *in situ*
Canterbury bell (*Campanula medium*)	mid-summer; blue, white, pink, purple	90 × 30cm (36 × 12in)	late spring	mid-summer	
Double daisy (*Bellis perennis flore-pleno*)	late spring–mid-autumn; white, pink, red, crimson	7.5 × 10cm (3 × 4in)	late spring	mid–late summer	
Forget-me-not (*Myosotis scorpioides*)	mid–late spring; blue, red	12.5 × 20cm (5 × 8in)	early–mid-summer		15cm (6in) apart
Foxglove (digitalis)	late spring–early summer, white, pink, purple, apricot, cream, yellow	90–150 × 30–37.5cm (36–60 × 12–15in)	late spring	mid–late summer	
Hollyhock (*Althaea rosa*)	mid–late summer; red, pink, yellow, salmon	150–180 × 60–75cm (60–72 × 24–30in)	late spring–early summer	mid–late summer	
Sweet William	early–late summer; red, white, purple, salmon, crimson	15–45 × 30cm (6–18 × 12in)	late spring–early summer	mid–late summer	
Verbascum bombyciferum (mullein)	early–mid-summer; yellow; large, grey, very furry leaves, furry stems	150 × 90cm (60 × 36in)	late spring–early summer		
Wallflower	mid-spring–early summer; yellow, red, brown, orange, wine, crimson, cream, rose, purple	37.5–60 × 20–30cm (15–24 × 8–12in)	late spring–early summer	either transplant mid–late summer, or thin *in situ*	

Greenhouse: *Campanula isophylla* Christmas cactus Chrysanthemum Cyclamen Freesia Fuschia Pelargonium (zonal)

bonding effect, start alternate lines with half a turf. All this will ensure quick and successful knitting of the turves.

As you work, use a standing board to avoid compaction of the soil or turves; when the job is finished, do not use a roller, but fill in the cracks with topdressing mixture or coarse sand, brushing it in as you go. Make sure that all the edges finish with full size turves, not narrow strips, otherwise the edge will be ragged and messy. Push soil up against the outside turves when laid; this prevents the exposed face of the turf drying out and becoming uneven.

Mowing
Established lawns may need one last light cut; turfed lawns can be topped, if required, two or three weeks after laying and a lawn from seed sown in early autumn may just need its first cut, as advised in mid-spring.

Stopping
Sweetpea seedlings which have not been so treated should have the growing tip removed just above the third pair of leaves (see Mid-Autumn).

Protecting
Rock plants with woolly or grey leaves will need a cover against winter wet; it is not so much cold which kills them as sodden roots and repeatedly soaked leaves. A gravel mulch round the plants to keep the leaves off the soil and cloches above them will keep them in good condition through the winter. Cloches put over the Christmas roses, too, will encourage them to unfold their petals and keep them free of mud. Agapanthus will be the better for a 15cm (6in) deep mulch of leaves, straw, peat or bracken and kniphofia can be treated similarly, to ensure their certain survival.

Tidying/sweeping

The leaves start to come down with a vengeance in late autumn, and it is even more vital to clear them off lawns, especially newly sown ones, and off small plants, whether seedlings, rock plants or herbaceous plants. Get them out of the pool, too, and collect them off drives and paths before they begin to rot and become dangerously slippery. In general, there will be an over-all clearing up of rubbish blown about by autumn gales.

Lighting

Christmas-flowering bulbs should be brought into light during late autumn when about 2.5cm (1in) of leaf and flower bud is showing and treated as specified by the nurseryman who supplied them. In general, they should be kept cool, at about 7°C (45°F) for the first few days while the leaves become green, and then given warmth gradually, with as much light as possible.

Cutting down

As the earliest of the late-flowering chrysanthemums finish blooming, the stems should be cut back to leave about 7.5cm (3in) of stump and the crowns in their pots put under the staging, for the time being, keeping the compost just moist.

Greenhouse work

As the light becomes less, in quantity and quality, with the approach of the end of the year, the glazing should be kept clean and clear of condensation at all times. Artificial heat will be needed most of the time, but not much ventilation, just enough to prevent a 'stuffy' atmosphere. Water in the mornings only, if needed, remove fallen and decaying vegetation and watch for missed pockets of greenfly or whitefly, especially on fuchsias, cinerarias and cyclamen. The greenhouse in winter is a haven for pests and diseases and is the one place where you will still have to be really vigilant.

A new strain of smaller flowered, fragrant cyclamen is now available for growing in pots, to flower at Christmas.

Plants in flower

Chrysanthemum (Korean), Violet

In unusual conditions

Bergenia, Michaelmas Daisy, Polyanthus, Primula, Christmas rose (Helleborus niger)

Greenhouse

Campanula isophylla (Italian bell flower)
Christmas cactus,
Chrysanthemum, Cyclamen,
Freesia, Fuchsia,
Pelargonium (zonal)

Early Winter

It is a debatable point whether early winter or mid-winter is the quietest season in the flower garden: probably mid-winter, since that is when snow or hard frost tends to make it impossible to do any cultivation. In such weather plants certainly will not be growing and the majority of the herbaceous types will be underground, well out of the way of trouble.

Early winter, however, is still likely to have relatively reasonable weather; there may be some very wet days, and occasional frosty nights, but it should still be possible to get out and do some cultivation and some final tidying up. The grass can be lightly mown on established lawns and turf can be laid for new ones. Lawns seeded in the autumn may also need some attention.

It is a good season to undertake major construction jobs, such as building a rock garden, starting an excavation for a pool or re-designing the layout of beds and borders. Woodwork for the garden, such as pergolas, fences, arches and supports for climbers can be made and put into position and repairs done to any which already exist. However, any work which involves the making and laying of concrete should wait; because of the risk of frost, it is not a winter job and should be fitted in, if possible, with the summer or early autumn work.

The warmth in the greenhouse will ensure that there is still growing life in there and besides plants currently in flower, there will be others coming on for the weeks after Christmas and the beginning of spring. These will all need attention on most days and the greenhouse environment itself needs careful management, juggling with the necessities of warmth, light, ventilation and water and at the same time warding off pest attack. Plants in frames should not be forgotten; although hardier, they also need light, fresh air and protection from the coldest frosts.

At~a~glance diary

Dig: sites intended for herbaceous perennial beds and borders, spring-sown hardy annuals and bedding plants to be planted late spring, spring-sown lawn from seed, nursery bed and cold frame, sweetpea trenches

Construct: rock garden

Turf: lawn

Mow: established lawns, new lawns lightly

Light: winter-flowering bulbs, Christmas cactus

Cut back: late-flowering chrysanthemums

Greenhouse and cold frame: ventilate, water, protect from cold

Increase: mid-autumn and late-autumn-flowering chrysanthemums from cuttings

Routine work: break any ice on pools; clear and tidy lawns, beds, paths, over-wintering annuals and biennials; overhaul tools and machinery

Pests and diseases: slugs, greenfly, red spider mite, whitefly

Jobs to do

Digging

The general digging that was described in late autumn can be continued or started while the weather permits, in early winter; this includes the preparation of beds for herbaceous perennials and borders, sweetpea trenches, sites for spring-sown hardy annuals and bedding and half-hardy annuals to be planted late in spring next year. You can also do the basic digging for a lawn to be sown in spring, leaving the surface rough over winter. It is probable that the weed seeds will not germinate as well in the interim as they would with a summer fallowing, but with a hard enough frost some seeds, especially those near the surface, may be killed.

If you have not already done so, early winter is a suitable time to choose a site for a nursery bed and prepare it. On it you can put a cold frame, a piece of equipment which has all sorts of uses. In order to avoid a lot of fetching and carrying, the nursery-bed should be next to or near the greenhouse. It should also be sheltered from wind, and from the north and east; it should receive both sun and shade. The soil needs to be especially good, well-drained and fertile, as it is to be used for seeds and growing on young plants before they are put into their permanent places. It is a good place to grow flowers for cutting too, so that the border is not vandalized by the flower arranger.

Frames can be used for hardening off plants, for sheltering real exotics during the summer, for containers of cuttings or seedlings or for direct planting. If for direct use, the base of the frame must be well drained. You may need to dig one or two spits deep, put in a layer of drainage material 5 or 7.5cm (2 or 3in) thick, then put on a covering of fibrous peat. Replace with only the topsoil if the subsoil is very heavy, and in that case bring up the level as required with additional compost mixture.

Construction

The shortage of space in many gardens ensures that tiny is beautiful; it is not essential to have lots of ground in order to enjoy gardening. You can get as much, if not more, pleasure out of a small rock garden and its plants and what

Phacelias are hardy annuals which originate in South and Central America. They are good bee flowers.

a big choice of plants there is, to provide you with flowers all through the growing season. The spring is generally known to be a rock garden's glory, but you can have a very good display of colour in summer and autumn; there are many small plants normally grown at the front of perennial borders which will fit equally well into a miniature alpine landscape.

The one thing above all else that rock garden plants must have is good drainage: whether you are dealing with a natural slope or producing an artificial mound, make sure that the subsoil is well-drained, mixing coarse grit with it if heavy. If it is really sticky subsoil, such as clay, it will have to be dug out, a spit deep, drainage material put in, and replaced with good topsoil mixed with grit. Ideally, rock-garden soil should be at least 60cm (2ft) deep and a good mixture would contain 3 parts loam, 2 parts peat or leaf-mould and 1 part grit (parts by bulk).

In a well-planned rock garden, the building is done from the bottom up, putting base layers of rock or stone first, adding soil, then planting and finally starting another layer. The rocks should be arranged to look as though they were there naturally and not artificially put into position; this natural look can be partly obtained by making sure the strata of any type of rock all run the same way. Each piece should be set into the soil so that it slopes back slightly, to ensure its permanence in that position and the drainage of rain off it, back into the soil.

When you are placing the rocks, remember that some plants like sun and some like shade, and construct crevices and gullies, as well as plateaux and peaks. The finished article should look as though you built the rest of the garden round it like a natural hump or bank, through which the underlying bed rocks are protruding due to centuries of soil erosion.

Two types of rock, sandstone and limestone, are most suitable and choice of either or both depends on the nature of your soil and therefore the kinds of plants you wish to grow. Sandstone is more likely to be acid in reaction; limestone is definitely alkaline and some rock plants (like other types of plants) are lime-haters. Hence a test of your soil (see liming, Mid-Winter) and an hour or so with a catalogue of alpine plants can save you a good deal of money and future frustration.

Left: *Build a rock garden from the bottom up, starting with a base layer of rock or grit and adding soil. Each piece of rock should slope backward slightly, so that rain drains off it, back into the soil, and so that it stays in position. The rocks should look as natural as possible.*

Limnanthes douglasii, *too, is attractive to bees, and will self-seed, to flower in autumn as well as late spring.*

Turfing
Lawns can be made from turf laid in early winter, as well as in late autumn, if weather and soil conditions permit (see Late Autumn for method).

Mowing
Although not generally realized, it is possible to cut the lawn during winter, under certain conditions. It does grow at this time, albeit very slowly, and becomes somewhat shaggy; you can take the top off it to leave it 4-5cm (1½-2in) long. The best time is the middle of a sunny day, not frosty, and preferably when the ground is as firm as it is likely to be in winter. Wet grass cannot be cut, as it becomes torn, and wet soil is soft, with the result that the mower gouges tracks in it. Top the grass of a lawn seeded in early autumn, if it has not yet been cut.

Bringing plants into light and warmth
Bulbs for flowering at Christmas and in mid-winter should be brought out into light as soon as possible (see Late Autumn), and the Christmas cactus can now come into

warmth, whether the greenhouse or the home. This will bring on its flower-buds very quickly; to time flowering to coincide with Christmas Day in the Northern Hemisphere, bring the plants in the second week of early winter.

Breaking ice
If you have a pool with fish in it and it becomes completely frozen over in cold weather, break the ice gently to make a small hole and let in fresh air, and therefore oxygen. Non-tropical fish will be safe in cold weather, provided oxygen is available in the water.

Clearing and tidying
Rake off any remaining leaves from grass, beds, paths and overwintering annuals and biennials, fork up established herbaceous perennial borders and work in a little bonemeal at 90g per sq m (3oz per sq yd) if not done in late autumn. Brush seedling lawns gently.

Cutting back
Continue to cut down the late-flowering chrysanthemums as the blooms finish and put under the greenhouse staging temporarily until they begin to produce new shoots. Keep the compost moist.

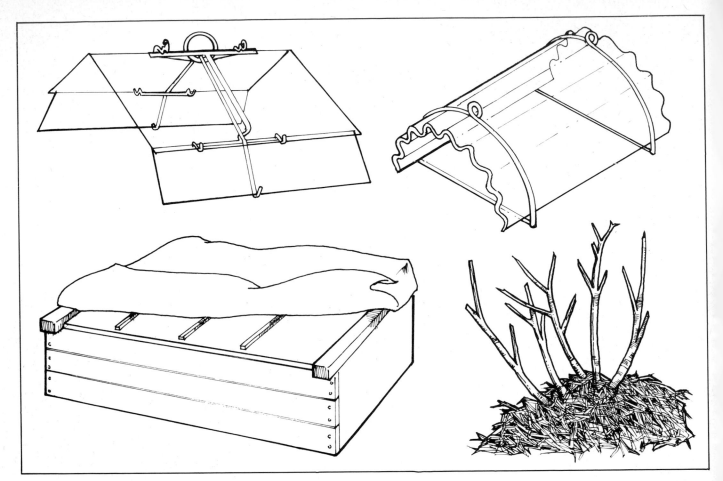

Greenhouse and frame management

Be prepared for sudden, considerable drops in temperature at night and boost the heating in the greenhouse as necessary. Cover the frame light on particularly cold nights with sacking or other protective material. Also be prepared to decrease the heating on sunny, calm days and then open the ventilators as well and let in some much-needed fresh air. Wipe off condensation and water plants moderately. Keep house and frame free of dead plants, rotting leaves, and dying flowers and supply final support strings for the corm-grown freesias, which will be coming into flower soon. *Primula malacoides* and possibly *P. obconica* will be flowering in mid-winter, so their buds will be starting to show and they may need a little more water than previously.

Increasing

Cuttings of chrysanthemums which flowered in late autumn may be ready for taking at the end of early winter, though mid-winter is more likely. Shoots will have been produced from below the soil round the old stems, since

Above: *Protection for grey- or woolly-leaved rock plants can be provided by cloches of glass or plastic ; a frame with sacking on top is an alternative for slightly tender pot plants ; a 15cm (6in) mulch will protect crowns of tender perennials.*
Opposite: *The blazing sunshine yellow of chrysanthemum Cloth of Gold lights up the garden in autumn.*

they were cut back, and these should be used, not the shoots actually growing on the stems, or any produced while the plants were still flowering.

Overhauling machinery and tools

A cold job, but a necessary one, conveniently done in winter, is cleaning and repairing garden tools and equipment. Inevitably, if you leave the sharpening of the mower blades and the servicing of the cultivator, hedge cutter, etc., until early spring, everyone else in the district will do the same and the delay until you get them back from the repair or maintenance centre can mean the ruin of the lawn and failure with crops and flowers for the season.

Annual climbing plants like the Morning Glory are 'instant' sources of colourful cover for vertical space.

Plants in flower

Christmas rose (Helleborus niger) Violet

In unusual conditions

Bergenia, Iris reticulata, Polyanthus, Primrose, Snowdrop

Greenhouse

Christmas cactus, Chrysanthemum, Cyclamen, Freesia, Fuchsia, Pelargonium (zonal)

Hand tools should automatically be cleaned after use during the growing season, but in winter, oiling them is advisable while they are not needed for some time. You can take the opportunity now to sharpen spades, billhooks, shears – all tools with cutting edges in fact – to straighten teeth, strengthen handles and tighten screws, nuts and bolts. Wheelbarrows in particular take a lot of punishment; oiling the wheels, patching holes in the body and padding the handles are usually the most important attentions needed.

Treating pests and diseases
Slugs are possible round the Christmas rose, so discourage them with 15cm (6in) bands of coarse grit round the plants or with slug-bait. Greenfly, whitefly and red spider mite may be persisting in the snug atmosphere of the greenhouse; either use finger and thumb or an insecticide (see Flower Garden Controls and Treatments for chemicals).

Mid-Winter

The best that can be said about mid-winter, as far as the weather is concerned, is that the days are beginning to lengthen, so that there is at least more light, even if the temperature is low. Light is more important to green plants than warmth; without light they cannot live at all, but they will survive or grow slowly in relatively cold conditions, provided light is available. Hence the flowering of snowdrops, *Iris reticulata*, bergenias and some other tough herbaceous plants which have adapted to cold.

Hard frost, heavy rain and snow are all likely through mid-winter and you should not expect to be able to do much gardening, beyond small routine jobs in the greenhouse. Occasionally lawns can have a little work done on them; lime can be spread if needed, digging can be finished and occasional tidying is possible, on sunny, frosty days, of the results of winter gales.

Otherwise you can spend your time in the greenhouse or in an armchair planning your next growing season, with the seductive help of the new seed catalogues. It is a good time to take stock of your flowering display all round, including perennials, bulbs, annuals, bedding plants and rock plants. With experience you can arrange a continual show of flowers from early spring until winter; even in winter there are a few plants which will flower. Really, there is no end to the flowering season, merely a diminution at certain times.

Your efforts last summer in starting various plants from seed in containers will begin to show from now until early spring and you should have quite a lot of colour as well as fragrance in the greenhouse from flowering pot plants. A gently heated greenhouse in mid-winter is a great morale booster, as it can be the source of so much colour and the promise of spring for remarkably little expense, if you use paraffin heaters.

At~a~glance diary

Dig: finish all digging

Lime: soil which is very acid, or soil which is very heavy, where plants need slightly alkaline rather than slightly acid soils

Feed: spring-flowering bulbs

Mow: established lawns, lawns grown from autumn-laid turf, lightly

Pot: rooted chrysanthemum cuttings

Start: early-flowering chrysanthemums to provide cuttings

Sterilize: loam needed for use in composts in late winter and onwards

Greenhouse: ventilate, water, heat, treat pests and diseases

Increase: late-flowering chrysanthemums from stem cuttings; gaillardia, phlox and oriental poppy from root cuttings

Routine work: break any ice on pools; plan and choose plants for the new season, and re-design the garden layout where necessary

Jobs to do

The petunia is one of the best plants for window-boxes and troughs, provided that it has plenty of sun.

Digging

Finish this as soon as possible as there is only just enough time left for the cultivated ground to be weathered sufficiently before the spring planting starts. Take advantage of hard frozen ground to wheel and place barrow-loads of organic matter, ready for mixing in when a thaw comes.

Liming

The addition of chalk to the soil of the ornamental garden is not as important as with the kitchen garden, but no plant likes extreme acid conditions; most of them will grow best in soils which have a pH of 6.0-6.5, i.e. slightly acid. Some do better with a little alkalinity, of about 7.3-7.5. A test to discover the value of your soil is easily done and you can buy the materials for it in a kit, complete with instructions, from any good garden sundriesman.

A word about pH – it may sound mysterious and complicated, but as far as gardeners are concerned, all that it is, is a measure of how acid or alkaline the soil is. The reason for needing to know this is that, in very alkaline soils, some mineral nutrients – iron and magnesium are two – are present in a chemical form which makes it impossible for the roots of certain plants to absorb them. These plants are what is known as calcifuges and have to be grown in acid-reacting soils, if they are grown at all. The pH scale of acidity/alkalinity runs from 0-14; the lower figures show acidity, decreasing until they get to 7.0, which is the neutral point. After that increasing alkalinity is indicated up to the maximum of 14.0. In practice, most garden soils show a reaction somewhere between 5.0 and 7.5-8.0.

Besides altering the pH of the soil, lime has an effect on the soil structure, especially of heavy soils, and makes them easier to deal with and much less likely to be permanently saturated. Gypsum (calcium sulphate) is a particular form of lime which will break down such soils without altering the pH value, as it is neutral, and is particularly useful where the soil is heavy but already alkaline. Use a soil tester to find out whether this is the case in your garden.

There are various sorts of lime to use, the most common

Most scillas are deep blue, but S. tubergeniana *is a very pale blue. It grows to about 15cm (6in) in height.*

being chalk or ground limestone; both are calcium carbonate, ground limestone being slower in its action. Hydrated lime (calcium hydroxide) can also be applied; it acts more quickly. Rates of application will be given with the lime containers or with the soil-testing kit. Lime must always be put on with an interval of several weeks between its application and that of organic matter, to avoid a chemical reaction between them which results in the loss of plant foods.

Feeding

Although it seems an unlikely time to supply food to plants, the spring-flowering bulbs – such as daffodils, scillas and crocus – will have poked through the soil by an inch or two. They at least are active and, provided snow is not lying several inches deep, the ground is not hard with frost or sodden with moisture, they will appreciate a boost in the form of a general compound fertilizer at 90-120g per sq m (3-4oz per sq yd).

Plants are like other living organisms: they need food, not in solid form as with animals, but in the liquid state. The food they absorb from the soil consists of various mineral elements: phosphorus, potassium, sulphur and so on, each of which has a different function in the plant's metabolism. In order that the plants can 'eat' them, these minerals must be broken up into minute particles which become part of the soil moisture and form a solution with it.

This solution passes into the plant roots, and from there to the other parts, the stem, the leaves and the flowers in particular, and the minerals then interact with the results of the process, known as photosynthesis, which goes on in the green tissue of plants.

Each mineral nutrient has a chemical symbol, for instance phosphorus is P, potassium K and nitrogen N. A packet of fertilizer will have the 'analysis' of the contents on it, that is, the mineral nutrients present and their percentage in the fertilizer will be shown: for example, Nitrogen, N, 7%, Phosphorus, P_2O_5, 4% and Potassium, K_2O, 9%. The phosphorus and potassium have to be present as compounds for technical reasons; in this analysis the potassium present is slightly more than the nitrogen, which would be good for flowering. More nitrogen would favour leaves and a higher proportion of phosphorus would encourage root growth. These three nutrients are the ones usually given as a supplement to organic matter, as they are the most important ones to plants, but others can be obtained and used if need be.

If plants do not have the mineral foods they need they show various symptoms of ill-health and will die if the deficiencies are acute or continue for long enough. However, the average garden soil, provided it is kept in good condition by the regular addition of rotted organic matter and an occasional application of proprietary fertilizers, should not lack the various minerals needed and discolorations of leaves are more likely to be the result of infections.

Mowing
It is unlikely that the next few weeks will be suitable for mowing, or even topping the grass, but occasionally a mild mid-winter occurs, when the birds sing, the sun shines and all sorts of plants show signs of growth, lulled into believing that spring has arrived. In such conditions, topping can be done, of established lawns, or those grown from autumn-laid turf, if it has put on some growth (see Early Winter for details).

Breaking
Watch the pool for a solid sheet of ice and remember that taking a hammer to it will sound like an explosion to the fish beneath; melt a hole in it if it is really thick.

Potting
Any late-flowering chrysanthemum cuttings taken in early winter should have rooted by mid-winter and will be ready for potting some time during this season. They can be transferred to individual 5 or 7.5cm (2 or 3in) diameter pots

of J.I. No. 1 potting compost and, as a precaution, you can keep them in the propagating frame (but without extra warmth), or put plastic bags over each pot for two or three days, while they settle.

Starting
Early-flowering chrysanthemum crowns (stools) which have been overwintering in a cold frame may just be starting to produce new growth, so they can be encouraged by moderate watering near the end of mid-winter.

Nemesias are half-hardy annuals in all colours, including blue. They flower continuously throughout the summer.

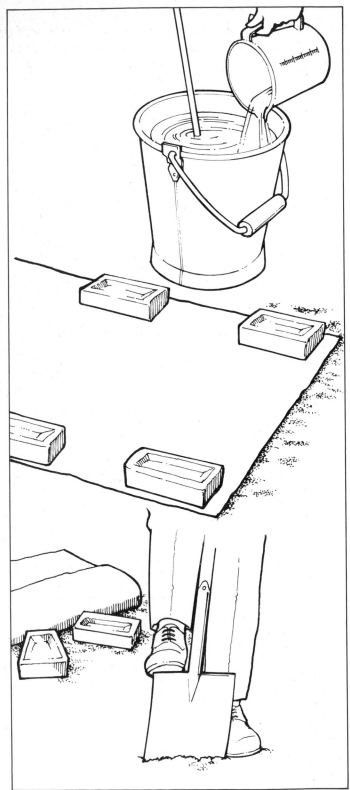

Sterilizing

Unless you are buying seed and potting composts made up ready for use, you will need to sterilize the loam for them early in mid-winter. It is then certain to be entirely free from the sterilizing agent when needed in late winter. A formalin solution is the most effective, the dilution rate with water being 1 part formalin in 49 parts water; 9L (2 gal) will treat 36L (1 bushel) of loam. The best method is to spread the loam out in a thin layer on a hard surface, water it well with the solution, mound it up into a heap and then cover to trap the fumes for 48 hours. After this it can be spread out thinly again and left to dry; allow three to four weeks at least for the fumes to evaporate entirely. Once the loam no longer smells of formalin, it is safe to use. Do not do the sterilizing in the greenhouse; formalin and its fumes are lethal to plant life. Peat and sand are already inert, and do not need sterilizing.

Greenhouse work

Continue to remove condensation from the inside of the greenhouse and leaves from the outside, to let in as much light as possible. You may have bonus light in the form of reflected light from snow. Keep the temperature as even as possible, not lower then 7°C (45°F) at night and 10-16°C (50-60°F) during the day, give a little ventilation during the day and shut down early in the afternoon, to retain as much of any sun warmth as possible. Water plants very carefully; give them just enough to wet the compost evenly all the way through and then leave them alone until the surface looks dry. At this time of the year, plants are touchy about their water needs: the amount should be exactly right.

Increasing

You can continue to take cuttings from the cut-down late-autumn and early winter-flowering chrysanthemums until the end of mid-winter, and start with those produced by the early to mid-autumn-flowering kinds.

You can also use the roots of certain plants for cuttings; phlox, Oriental poppies and gaillardia are some. Phlox tend to suffer from a pest called stem and leaf eelworm, but if you increase the plants from root cuttings you avoid this trouble. Perfectly healthy plants can be produced from infested plants by this method of increase.

Left: *Sterilizing soil. Mix formalin with water, taking care not to inhale the vapour, saturate soil and cover for 4-8 hours, then turn and use when all smell has been dissipated.* Opposite: *Many border flowers can look rather ragged by late summer but perennial phlox are at their best then.*

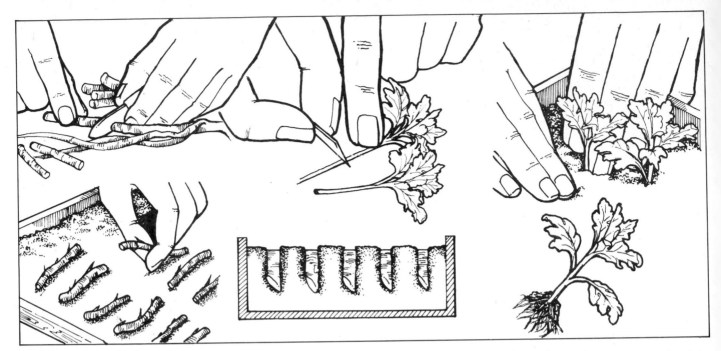

Taking cuttings: Roots are cut into 5cm (2in) lengths and put vertically in, or on top of, the compost. Chrysanthemum cuttings are taken from crown shoots, not stem shoots. Below: Busy lizzies (impatiens)—the outdoor kinds—are superb plants for providing colour on shady patios.

The roots are cut up into pieces about 2.5-5cm (1-2in) long; those from the poppies are put vertically into compost, the others laid horizontally on the surface and covered about 0.6cm ($\frac{1}{4}$in) deep. Kept in the gently heated greenhouse, they will root slowly, shoots will begin to appear and you can plant them out late in spring in their permanent positions after hardening off.

Planning and choosing

All the best seasonal gardening books insist that the well-organized gardener does his or her garden designing and selection of plants in the depth of winter, partly because it helps to supply text at a time of year when there is little work to discuss. Nevertheless, it has to be admitted that midwinter is a convenient time to take stock; for one thing, this is when the new seed catalogues are published, well in advance of the growing season. Since there actually is not very much to do outdoors and since spring, summer and autumn are times when you need running boots, the only peace you will have to consider and re-plan is the time when plant dormancy and hibernation have set in.

You could also make a resolution to keep a garden notebook. Details about times of sowing and planting, crop and flower yields, cultivations done, plant troubles, when pests and disease appeared and how you dealt with them, weed control and, above all, detailed daily notes about the weather, will all provide an extremely useful and entertaining garden work reference in future. Moreover, it will help to

Half-hardy Annuals and Bedding Plants

All should be sown in a temperature of 13–16°C (55–60°F) in early spring, pricked out in mid-spring and planted out in late spring–early summer

Name	Time of flowering; flower colour	Height and spread cm/in	Type of flower
Ageratum	mid–late summer; blue, white	10–22.5 × 10–17.5cm (4–9 × 4–7in)	brush
Antirrhinum	early summer–early autumn; yellow, red, orange, pink, white, wine, salmon, bronze	10–90 × 7–37.5cm (4–36 × 3–15in)	two-lipped, carried in spikes
Aster	late summer–early autumn; pink, mauve, lavender, rose, white, yellow, cream	15–75 × 10–30cm (6–30 × 4–12in)	daisy
Begonia	mid-summer–early autumn; pink, red	22.5 × 20cm (9 × 8in)	flat panicles
Cosmos	early–late summer; pink, red, white, orange, yellow, crimson; fern-like leaves	45–90 × 20–30cm (18–36 × 8–12in)	daisy
Dahlia	mid-summer–mid-autumn; all colours but blue	30–45 × 20–25cm (12–18 × 8–10in)	daisy or double forms
Helichrysum (everlasting)	mid–late summer; red, yellow, pink, crimson, orange, rose	30–75 × 17.5–22.5cm (12–30 × 7–9in)	daisy
Impatiens	mid-summer–early autumn; pink, orange, red white, salmon	15–22.5 × 10–15cm (6–9 × 4–6in)	flat saucer
Limonium (statice, sea-lavender, everlasting)	mid–late summer; lavender, pink, dark blue, yellow	45–60 × 20cm (18–24 × 8in)	spike
Lobelia	mid-summer–mid-autumn; blue, red, purple, white, wine	10–22.5 × 10–15cm (4–9 × 4–6in)	tubular or flat
Marigold, French and African	mid-summer–early autumn; bronze, deep red, orange, yellow	15–90 × 10–37.5cm (6–36 × 8–15in)	daisy, ball
Mesembryanthemum (Livingstone daisy)	mid–late summer; salmon, cream, magenta, rose, white, carmine	7–10 × 20cm (3–4 × 8in)	daisy
Nemesia	early summer–early autumn; red, yellow, orange, white, crimson, bronze, cerise, pink, blue	15–30 × 10–15cm (6–12 × 4–6in)	trumpet
Petunia	mid-summer–early autumn; rose, white, pink, blue, purple, red	15–30 × 10–20cm (6–12 × 4in)	flat
Portulaca	mid–late summer; yellow, red, white, magenta, orange, rose	15 × 10cm (6 × 4in)	saucer-shaped
Salvia	mid-summer–early autumn; red, purple, violet-blue	30–37.5 × 30cm (12–15 × 12in)	spike
Senecio (cineraria)	grown for silver-grey leaves	22.5–30 × 30cm (9–12 × 7–8in)	insignificant
Stock, double and East Lothian	early summer–mid-autumn; pink, white, lavender, rose, mauve, crimson; fragrant	37.5–60 × 12–20cm (15–24 × 5–8in)	spike
Tobacco plant (Nicotiana)	early summer–early autumn; white, yellow, red, rose, mauve, crimson, lime-green	25–90 × 15–25cm (10–36 × 6–10in)	tubular
Zinnia	late summer–early autumn; all colours but blue	15–90 × 15–30cm (6–36 × 6–12in)	ball or daisy

A well-grown bed of tobacco plants (nicotiana). These subtly-coloured flowers perfume the air heavily in the evening.

explain a good many otherwise inexplicable failures or successes, and to prevent the repetition of mistakes.

The length of time it takes for various seeds to germinate is an extremely useful piece of information which is hard to come by and a note about whether they germinate better in darkness or light is another.

Setting up a table to show the times of flowering of perennials, bulbs and so on, will show you where the gaps are in continuity of blooming. It is, incidentally, an eye-opener as to how useful various plants are. Some may be literally continuously in flower for eight weeks or more; others, very showy and popular, may last only two or three weeks and take up room for the remaining fifty weeks of the year without paying their way by having attractive foliage or growth habit.

An experimental gardener cannot do without a notebook if he or she has set up comparisons between various methods of cultivation or control of troubles, or hybridizing programmes, and the notebook can be made visually interesting with sketches, paintings or photographic prints.

All in all, the winter, if not physically active, can be mentally busy and suddenly, without any help from you, you will find the snowdrops are in flower, the aconites are shining in a corner and the time for sitting is past.

Plants in flower

Bergenia,
Christmas rose (Helleborus niger),
Eranthis (winter aconite),
Iris reticulata,
Iris unguicularis,
Snowdrop, Violet

Greenhouse

Christmas cactus, Cyclamen,
Freesia, Hyacinth (treated),
Narcissus,
Primula obconica,
Primula malacoides

Late Winter

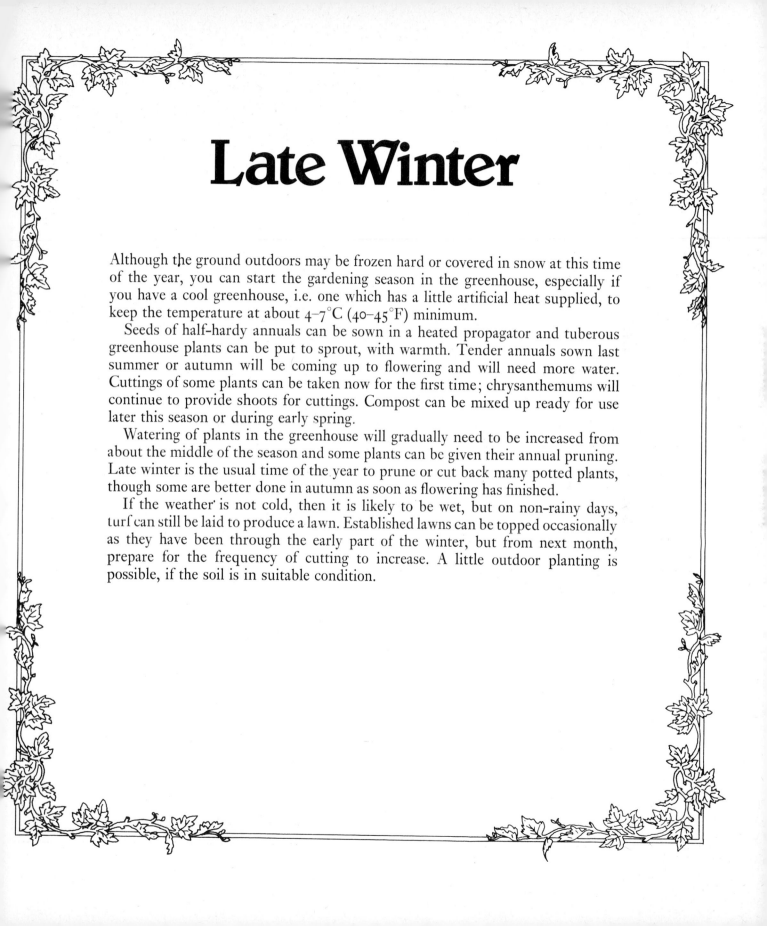

Although the ground outdoors may be frozen hard or covered in snow at this time of the year, you can start the gardening season in the greenhouse, especially if you have a cool greenhouse, i.e. one which has a little artificial heat supplied, to keep the temperature at about 4–7°C (40–45°F) minimum.

Seeds of half-hardy annuals can be sown in a heated propagator and tuberous greenhouse plants can be put to sprout, with warmth. Tender annuals sown last summer or autumn will be coming up to flowering and will need more water. Cuttings of some plants can be taken now for the first time; chrysanthemums will continue to provide shoots for cuttings. Compost can be mixed up ready for use later this season or during early spring.

Watering of plants in the greenhouse will gradually need to be increased from about the middle of the season and some plants can be given their annual pruning. Late winter is the usual time of the year to prune or cut back many potted plants, though some are better done in autumn as soon as flowering has finished.

If the weather is not cold, then it is likely to be wet, but on non-rainy days, turf can still be laid to produce a lawn. Established lawns can be topped occasionally as they have been through the early part of the winter, but from next month, prepare for the frequency of cutting to increase. A little outdoor planting is possible, if the soil is in suitable condition.

At~a~glance diary

Prepare compost for: sowing seed and potting under glass

Sow seeds under glass(in heat)of: ageratum, antirrhinum, fibrous-rooted and tuberous begonia, cosmos, dahlia, gloxinia (sinningia), impatiens, lobelia, mesembryanthemum, nemesia, petunia, dwarf phlox, portulaca, salvia, senecio, streptocarpus, ursinia

Pot: rooted cuttings of chrysanthemum, gaillardia and oriental poppy, schizanthus, hippeastrum

Prune, cut back: fuchsia, hoya, passion flower, pelargonium, tradescantia family and other climbing, trailing or shrubby plants

Increase: early-and late-flowering chrysanthemums from cuttings

Start: achimenes, large-flowered tuberous begonia, gloxinia (sinningia), streptocarpus

Greenhouse: water, ventilate and tidy

Routine work: brush and top established lawns, lay turf for new lawns, plant florists' anemones, weed and clear up generally

Jobs to do

Preparing compost for sowing seed under glass

If you have not very much time, you can buy these composts ready made up, but the advantages of making them up yourself are that you do know exactly what ingredients have been used in them, and they cost less. You should never use garden soil for container-grown plants; the alterations in aeration and drainage of the growing medium produced by the physical restrictions of containers result in poor root growth. Composts contain a mixture of ingredients balanced in their proportions and chemical contents so that the plant roots can develop to their maximum.

This rock garden dianthus, La Bourbille, grows only 7.5-15cm (3-6in) tall: one of the best flowering rock plants.

You will need both seed and potting composts and you can use those that contain soil or the more modern soil-less ones. One of the most commonly used composts is the one called John Innes; this can be bought ready-mixed for use. However, for home mixing you will need the following: 2 parts sterilized loam, 1 part granulated peat and 1 part coarse silver sand (all parts by bulk). To each 36L (1 bushel) of mixture, add 45g (1½oz) superphosphate and 21g (¾oz)

The Christmas cactus will start to flower in early winter, provided that it is given short days from autumn onwards.

chalk and mix all the ingredients thoroughly together. They should be capable of passing through a 0.6cm ($\frac{1}{4}$in) sieve. This mixture is the John Innes Seed Compost.

The soil-less seed compost contains sphagnum peat and fine sand, usually in a 75:25 mixture, with lime and fertilizers added. There are many different formulae for these soil-less composts, depending on the plants and their needs and it is probably quicker and more satisfactory to buy them made up rather than make them up oneself and run the risk of damage to plants through wrong or excessive use of the ingredients. It is a matter of personal preference which you use, and you will probably find in time that you get better results with one or the other.

Preparing compost for potting

As with the seed composts, you can make up those needed for potting in advance; give them at least a week to mature before using and leave them in the greenhouse to warm up to the surrounding temperature.

The John Innes potting compost contains the following: 7 parts sterilized loam, 3 parts peat and 2 parts coarse sand (by bulk); to 36L (1 bushel) add 120g (4oz) of fertilizer made up as follows: 2 parts superphosphate, 2 parts hoof and horn meal and 1 part sulphate of potash (parts by weight). The compost should also have 21g ($\frac{3}{4}$oz) chalk added to every 36L (1 bushel).

This mixture is the J. I. Potting Compost No. 1; there are two more – No. 2 contains 240g (8oz) of fertilizer and 42g (1$\frac{1}{2}$oz) chalk per 36L (1 bushel), and No. 3 has 360g (12oz) of fertilizer and 63g (2$\frac{1}{4}$oz) of chalk per 36L (1 bushel). Some gardeners occasionally need a No. 4 mix, for certain very vigorous plants.

The No. 1 potting compost is used for small plants growing in pots from 5-10cm (2-4in) in diameter; No. 2 is suitable for those in pots from 12.5-17.5cm (5-7in), and No. 3 for the larger plants, in pots from 20cm (8in) in diameter and larger. However, this is not a rigid rule; fast-growing plants may need the No. 2 in a 10cm (4in) pot and No. 3 in a 17.5cm (7in) pot. Others flower better if slightly starved, so will be all right in No. 1 for longer, and you will be able to vary the composts as you gain experience.

There are soil-less potting composts, too, consisting of a peat and sand mixture, to which fertilizer and lime are added. Such composts for potting are not as useful, as they have much less in the way of food reserves. Because they are light in weight, the large and medium-sized plants are top-heavy and tend to fall over, but for small plants they can be ideal, as they are exceptionally well-aerated and drained; some plants grow better in them than in the John Innes type.

When you become experienced at container cultivation, you can vary the contents according to the plants you are growing, so that the composts are tailored exactly to the plants' needs. For instance, cacti, not surprisingly, thrive in gritty mixtures, so you can mix an extra part of very coarse sand or grit into the basic potting compost; pelargoniums naturally grow in poor but well-drained soils, so their composts can also be given more drainage material. For cactus seed, the J.I. seed compost with about $\frac{1}{4}$ part sand added to it will be good; they also germinate and grow surprisingly well in a soil-less seed compost – surprisingly, since their native habitat is gritty, to say the least.

Sowing seed in containers

Seed to sow in containers in late winter, during the last week, consists mainly of the half-hardy annuals and bedding plants: those which grow comparatively slowly and which are on the small side. Otherwise, by sowing at this time, you will be faced at the beginning of late spring with plants more than ready to be planted outdoors, when the weather may still be rather chilly, even for hardened-off plants. You can also sow seed of some tuberous plants: large-flowered begonias, dahlia, gloxinia (sinningia) and streptocarpus.

Wooden or plastic seed-trays are probably the most convenient containers to use, divided into sections, but pans are also very handy and, if any seeds are large, individual plastic, clay or peat pots can be used. Peat pots avoid the need for pricking out, as the whole pot can be planted or potted.

Fill the containers, press the compost down with the fingers at the sides and the corners first and then in the centre, and level the surface. Add more compost if necessary so that the final level is about 1cm (½in) below the top of the container and firm with a presser. Put partially in a tray of water so that the moisture is gradually drawn up through the compost; when the surface is obviously damp, remove the container and put to drain off the surplus water.

Sprinkle the seed evenly over the surface of the compost; if you sow it in clumps, the seedlings are more likely to be infected with damping-off, a damaging fungus disease. Sterilized loam avoids this, or watering them with a fungicide (see Flower Garden Controls and Treatments). Cover the seed with twice its own depth of compost, sieving it through a very fine sieve. If the seeds are minute, as begonia and cactus seeds are, don't cover them at all, simply press them into the surface. Cover the container with white plastic sheet, or brown paper and a sheet of glass, and put in a temperature of 16-18°C (60-65°F), away from the sun.

Sowing seed: Fill the seed-tray with seed compost and firm the corners and sides first; divide into sections to save on seed, label each section and sieve compost over seed. Cover with glass and newspaper until seed germinates.

You can vary these practices with experience; some seed germinates better in the light than in the dark and others need a higher temperature for germination or germinate more quickly with more warmth.

Potting
Plants needing potting now may be schizanthus, rooted chrysanthemum cuttings and root cuttings which have taken. The schizanthus sown in late summer should be put into their final 15cm (6in) size pots, if this has not already been done, potting them firmly and re-staking if necessary. Chrysanthemum cuttings taken in mid-winter will need potting, into 5 or 9cm (2 or 3½in) pots, depending on the root development, and root cuttings taken at the same time will need similarly-sized pots.

Hippeastrums can be retrieved from under the staging and started off again sometime during late winter. They quite often start themselves off, like cyclamen, but whatever state they are in, the compost can be watered moderately and the pots put on to the staging and into the propagator, if possible with a temperature of about 16°C (60°F). When the tip is obviously sprouting well, take them out of the propagator; the top 2.5cm (1in) of compost can then be removed and replaced with a topdressing of fresh. This can be done annually for three or four years before there is a need for complete repotting, as hippeastrums grow better if undisturbed. However, they do need regular feeding during the growing seasons when they are not repotted. Give them as much light as possible.

Pruning/cutting back greenhouse plants
Late winter is, in general, the best time to prune 'undercover' plants as early spring is when they start to grow again. In the cool greenhouse, the plants that will need pruning are climbers and fuchsias; pelargoniums can also be cut back now if they were not done last autumn.

Fuchsias should be pruned so that last summer's flowering shoots are cut back to leave one or two pairs of dormant buds, so that there is a kind of stub left. Older plants can have the main stem itself cut back by about half its length, to just above a good strong sideshoot, unless it is being grown as a standard. Short, thin shoots should be cut right off and the remainder thinned if crowded.

Left: *Hippeastrums, also sometimes called amaryllis, are tender bulbous plants for the greenhouse or home.*
Right: *Potting a hippeastrum. Use a 12cm (5in) pot, half fill with compost, centre the bulb on this and add further compost so that the bulb is half buried.*

Passion flowers can be pruned by removing all the weak shoots completely and cutting the strong shoots down to leave two-thirds of each stem. Hoya needs a little pruning to cut back straggling shoots to shape, and one or two of the oldest stems should be cut back by about a third. Trailing plants like tradescantias will probably need hard cutting as they are often very straggly at the end of the winter, so you can reduce the stems to about 7.5cm (3in) long. Pelargoniums can also be cut down hard, to leave stems about 10 or 12.5cm (4 or 5in) long. Remember that pruning cuts on all plants should always be made cleanly, just above a dormant bud or sideshoot, with no stub left.

Increasing
You can continue to take cuttings of late-flowering chrysanthemums and, throughout late winter, early-flowering kinds will be producing suitable new growth, especially if the weather is getting markedly warmer (see Mid-Winter for method).

Starting corms and tubers

Achimenes, large-flowering begonias, gloxinias (sinningias) and streptocarpus can all be encouraged to start growing by putting them into seed boxes containing moist peat. They should have the top of the corm or tuber just above the peat surface, except for the achimenes, which should be slightly below it. Space them out so that they do not touch one another. If you have room to put them in the propagator, they will come on more quickly.

General greenhouse work

Start watering plants which have been dormant; some may have already begun to grow, but only give moderate amounts at first, just enough to moisten the compost right through. Do not saturate it. Give a little more ventilation, especially on sunny days, when you can turn the heat off altogether in the middle of the day provided the temperature outside is above freezing. Tidy out the winter accumulation of debris, fallen or rotting leaves and stems, scrub any green mould off the outside of containers, brush down staging and floors and generally give the greenhouse a mild springclean.

Outdoor work

If the weather allows, top the lawn, brushing the grass first; also start a new lawn from turf (see Late Autumn for method). The tubers of the florists' anemones (St Brigid and de Caen strains) can be planted outdoors. Medium to light, sandy soil suits them and a sunny or lightly shaded position. Rotted organic matter should have been dug in some months earlier. Put the tubers 6.5-7.5cm (2½-3in) deep and about 15cm (6in) apart.

A general clearing up of leaves, twigs and other rubbish now will give you more time in spring; weeding can sometimes be done on fine days. Break the ice on pools if there are any fish in them and remove any leaves burying overwintering annuals.

Crocuses naturalized in light woodland follow the snowdrop as the first of the spring flowers.

Plants in flower
Bergenia, Crocus,
Eranthis (winter aconite),
Iris reticulata,
Iris unguicularis (syn. I. stylosa)
Snowdrop

In sheltered places
Anemone blanda, Chionodoxa,
Lenten rose (Helleborus orientalis),
Narcissi (miniature), Polyanthus,
Primrose, Pulmonaria (lungwort),
Scilla, Tulip (species)

Greenhouse
Cineraria, Freesia, Lachenalia,
Primula (from late-spring sowing)
Daffodils and Narcissi,
Hyacinth, Tulips (species)

Controls & Treatments

The gardener who is interested in herbaceous flowering plants is the one with the fewest problems of pest and disease control and treatment of various other plant ailments. There will certainly be some troubles but in a general way; greenfly, blackfly and caterpillars will always be found where there is plant life but, unlike vegetables and fruit, there are not a great many specific to certain plants. Leafminer on chrysanthemum and cineraria, rust on hollyhocks and antirrhinums, wilt on asters and pansies, earwigs on dahlias and some others are the exceptions that prove the rule.

You may find all through the season apparently mysterious brown spots and brown edges on leaves, holes and tattering on leaves and petals, stems broken and small plants laid completely flat. Most of this can be put down to the weather; wind, hail, sunscorch, frost, heavy rain and salt spray are all sources of damage, about which little can be done, and they are just the luck of the game. Well-grown, healthy plants, staked, fed and watered, will take such trials in their stride, reviving or producing new growth in no time.

A lack of one or more mineral nutrients in a plant will declare itself in the form of various discolorations on the leaves, stunting of plants and poor flowering. Such deficiency symptoms are not easily diagnosed accurately without professional help; they can be confused with symptoms of virus diseases, or with natural variegations in colour, yellow or cream in most cases, but consistently bad growth and flowering of plants on a particular piece of ground is a good guide. If manuring and feeding do not improve matters after a year or two, then ask for specialist advice. However, real deficiency troubles are rare in gardens; you are much more likely to be contending with pests and blight.

Virus diseases are a real but simple problem, once diagnosed; there is no cure, and infected plants should be destroyed as soon as possible before other plants are contaminated. Viruses consist of particles so small that they can only be seen with an electron microscope; these particles are present in the plant's sap and are absorbed by sucking insect pests (greenfly, capsids, etc.) as they feed. By then feeding on healthy plants, the insects spread the virus and another

One of the most convenient ways of applying a pesticide is as a powder from a puffer pack, aimed exactly where wanted.

plant is doomed. Irregular yellow patches, circles and lines on leaves, twisted growth, streaking or alteration of flower colour, and slowly lengthening, stunted shoots are indicators of viral infection but, like deficiency symptoms, are best confirmed by those trained to do so.

Insect and other pests attack in one of two ways: either by biting or by sucking. Caterpillars, maggots, slugs and snails all come into the former category, being armed with, if not actual teeth, mouthparts which can tear or rasp off relatively large pieces of leaf, flower or stem. They are sufficiently sizable to be hand-picked when seen; in really bad epidemics caterpillars and maggots can be sprayed with derris or fenitrothion. Slugs and snails should have slugbait containing methiocarb put down; they feed at night and need to be hunted with a torch for hand-picking.

The sucking insect pests such as aphids (greenfly, black-fly, root aphids, mealy aphid), capsids, thrips, leaf suckers and hoppers, whitefly, mealy bug, scale and red spider mite all pierce the plant tissue with needle-like mouthparts and draw up the sap through them. It therefore follows that insecticide sprayed on to the plant will be very effective and if absorbed into the plant's sap, even more so; such an insecticide is called systemic. This type of pest breeds extremely quickly and a plague will build up in a few weeks; although squashing with finger and thumb will help, other controls will generally be needed. Root aphids feed in the same way but below ground. Infested plants grow slowly, have a dull colour and wilt for no apparent reason. Derris and malathion are good general insecticides; bioresmethrin is good for aphids, whitefly (for which it was originally specified); dimethoate is best for dealing with capsid, mealy bug, leafminers and scale.

On lawns, one way of dealing with earthworms is to sprinkle derris powder well into the turf.

Woodlice frequently cause trouble by feeding on the roots of seedlings and young plants in pots and boxes, attacking them through the drainage holes. Move the containers frequently, raise them off the standing surface with pieces of wood or pot and dust the base with HCH (BHC).

But do remember that use of most of these insecticides harms the beneficial insects as well, including the pollinators such as bees and hover-flies. If you keep an observant eye on your plants, you can halt most of these pests before they get out of hand by killing the first one or two. Where one green-fly is obvious, there will be ten hidden, or there will be shortly, if you don't act immediately.

Grey mould (*Botytis cinerea*) infects through a previous injury and produces grey furry patches on leaves, stems and flowers, especially in cool, wet or humid conditions on practically any plant and can be treated with the systemic fungicide benomyl. Mildew produces white powder on leaves and flowers as well as buds and stems and causes most trouble from late summer onwards. Warmth, dewy nights and dry soil encourage its spread on plants; again use benomyl, or sulphur or dinocap.

Seedlings with stems reddish or black at soil level sometimes collapse; this is damping-off disease and is worst where seedlings are crowded. Use sterilized compost and water with Cheshunt compound to save remaining plants.

Weeds can cause a great deal of trouble in gardens but there are various modern chemical aids which kill them without harming cultivated plants growing nearby. Sodium chlorate is one which is watered in solution onto the soil so that it is absorbed by the plant roots; it remains effective for six months or more and is suitable for paths, drives, patios and all ground free of cultivated plants. Simazine is another of the same type, lasting twelve months, watered onto ground cleared of weeds, with the object of then keeping it clear. At certain dilution rates, recommended by the makers, it can be used round cultivated plants.

Dichlobenil is a third soil-acting weedkiller, applied dry in granular form to the soil to kill annual and perennial weeds. Like simazine, at certain application rates recommended by the makers, it can be used round some cultivated plants. It is effective for three to twelve months.

A second group of weedkillers consists of those sprayed on to the leaves and stems of weeds; they include those commonly known as 24D, 245T and MCPA. They are the so-called hormone weedkillers and will damage or kill any plant, not just weeds, as they are absorbed into the plant's sap, circulated round it and dislocate the normal working of its metabolism. Morfamquat is another of these, specific to weed seedlings growing in grass, so is used on newly germin-ated lawns; it is also effective on small-leaved weeds such as suckling clover or speedwell. Dalapon is also a translocated type, specific to couch grass and other grasses.

The latest weedkiller is glyphosphate, translocated, but not a hormone type. Sprayed on to the top growth, it deals with annuals and perennials but does not have its effect through plant roots.

A third type of weedkiller is that which is sprayed onto leaves and stems, but which only affects those containing chlorophyll – the green colouring matter of plants. It becomes inactivated on reaching the soil. For annual and small weeds it is very useful; paraquat and diquat are the chemical names. Directions for use of all these weedkillers must be read and followed for safe, satisfactory results.

Pests & Diseases

A bad attack of powdery mildew on chrysanthemums, which can be treated with benomyl or dinocap. This disease spreads rapidly in airless conditions and on plants short of water.

Pests and fungus diseases of particular plants
Antirrhinum
Rust: fungus disease. Symptoms are raised, bright rust-brown spots on undersurface of leaves and on stems; leaves wither. Some varieties are resistant; consult catalogues. Spray thiram at two-week intervals from end of early summer to end of late summer. Remove badly infected plants and burn.

Aster, annual
Aster wilt: soil-borne fungus disease which infects roots. Symptoms are wilting, then blackening of stems from base and browning of internal tissue of living stems. Wilt-resistant varieties are available; destroy infected plants, sterilize or replace soil.

Foot rot: soil-borne fungus disease which invades roots. Symptoms are blackening of base of stem, followed by sudden and total collapse of plant. Destroy infected plants, water soil round remaining plants with thiram or a copper-containing fungicide.

Begonia, see Cyclamen
Chrysanthemum
Leafminer: insect pest. Symptoms are wavy white lines on upper surface of leaves, in bad infestations leaves brown and wither. Hand-pick and spray with dimethoate; do not spray flowers.

Cineraria
Leafminer, see *Chrysanthemum*

Cyclamen
Vine weevil: insect pest. Symptoms are leaves wilting for no apparent reason, fat cream-coloured grubs in corms and compost. Adults are black, 0.6cm ($\frac{1}{4}$in) long, with a long, two-pronged snout; they eat holes in margins of leaves. Hand-pick grubs, water compost with HCH (BHC), trap adults in small pieces of rolled up sacking or paper placed on the soil.

Dahlia
Earwig: insect pest. Symptoms are holes and ragged edges to petals and leaves, flowers may then be infected with grey mould. Nocturnal feeder; trap in flower-pots stuffed with straw or paper, placed upside down on tops of stakes and spray plants and ground with trichlorphon or carbaryl.

Gladiolus
Thrips: insect pest. Symptoms are small silvery streaks on leaves and buds, later turning brown. Thrips are tiny, yellow-to-black pests, known as 'thunder bugs', most frequent during hot, dry weather. Remove affected buds, and spray with malathion.

Hollyhock

Hollyhock Rust: fungus disease. Spray thiram at two-week intervals from the end of early summer to the end of late winter. Remove badly infected plants and burn.

Hyacinth, see *Narcissus*

Lawn

Leather-jacket: insect pest. Symptoms are roundish patches of beige-coloured grass, slowly enlarging during late autumn, winter and spring. Grass is killed. Leather-jackets are grey-brown, slowly-moving caterpillars found in top 2.5cm (1in) or so of soil. Mature size is 2.5-3cm (1-1½in) long, adults are cranefly (daddy-long-legs). Water lawn with HCH (BHC) solution.

Fusarium patch: fungus disease (sometimes known as snow mould). Symptoms are pale yellow-brown patches of dead grass, edges sometimes fringed with white, fluffy growths. Disease most common autumn and winter. Remove infected areas, replace with fresh soil and turf or seed; water neighbouring turf with copper-containing fungicide.

Fairy ring: soil-borne fungus disease; symptoms are rings of toadstools in grass, 90cm (36in) and more in diameter. If grass within and around ring is dark green and does not die, spike 10cm (4in) deep and water with sulphate of magnesium at 60g in 4.5L per sq m (2oz in 1 gal per sq yd), two or three times at four or five-week intervals.

If the grass has died completely within ring, leaving a bare patch, remove soil and turf to a distance of 60cm (24in) beyond ring and a depth of 30-45cm (12-18in); replace with fresh, or sterilize the same area, forked up, with formalin, using a dilution rate of 1 part formalin to 39 parts water, and applying 18L per sq m (4gal per sq yd). Cover for ten days, then fork soil and replant when smell of formalin has gone (about six weeks).

Narcissus

Bulb fly: insect pest. Bulbs grow and flower poorly, do not flower at all, or die and do not appear in the season following infection. Bulbs become soft and contain white maggots internally. Destroy such bulbs and dust soil round remaining bulbs with HCH (BHC) from end of late spring at two-weekly intervals until end of early summer.

Pansy

Black-root rot: soil-borne fungus disease. Symptoms are yellowing leaves followed by withering, death of plant and blackening of roots. Destroy affected plants; rest soil for three years, or sterilize, or replace.

Stem rot: soil-borne fungus disease. Symptoms are yellowing of leaves which then die, main stem rots at base. Destroy affected plants; dust soil with fungicide containing mercury (calomel) and improve drainage, or plant in different site.

Pelargonium

Black-root rot, see *Pansy*; rust, see *Antirrhinum* (N.B., no resistant varieties of pelargonium).

Peony

Blight: fungus disease. Symptoms are wilting of plant and death of young shoots at base of main stem, following browning. Remove affected parts where possible. Treat plants and soil round them with benomyl fungicide; dig up and destroy plants if they do not recover and plant new specimens in a different site.

Bud disease: physiological. Symptoms are stem just below flower bud shrivelling and turning brown; bud hangs down and does not open. Supply potash in spring; make sure plant does not run short of water or become waterlogged. Protect from hot sun after cold nights.

Phlox

Eelworm: pest. Symptoms are twisted, narrow leaves, turning brown from base of plant and falling, stems swollen and splitting from base upwards, flowering poor or non-existent. Dig up plants in winter, use roots for cuttings, and destroy remainder of plant. Plant in different site.

Salpiglossis

Foot rot, see *Aster*

Stock

Wire-stem, see *Wallflower*

Sweetpea

Thrips, see *Gladiolus*; black-root rot, see *Pansy*

Tulip

Fire: fungus disease. Symptoms are blackened patches on leaf tips and later rest of leaf, and on buds and flowers; bulbs have blisters on the outside. Destroy badly infected plants; spray remainder and soil with captan or thiram, avoiding flowers. Following year start spraying when growth 2.5cm (1in) tall, until flowers unfold.

Violet

Leaf-midge: insect pest. Symptoms are thickened leaves, rolling inwards from margins. Plants small and poorly flowering. Pick off infested leaves and spray plant with dimethoate early in late spring, the middle of late summer and in mid-autumn.

Wallflower

Flea-beetle: insect pest. Symptoms are small round holes in leaves of seedlings and very young plants; tiny, hopping irridescent beetles present. Dust derris or HCH (BHC) on to leaves when dry.

Wire-stem: fungus disease. Symptoms are brown, constricted stem near base, plant stunted if not killed. Destroy infected plants; use sterilized soil for seed compost or seed-bed. Dust seed with captan or thiram.